The American West
1840-95

Design by John Rushton Associates
Picture research by Procaudio Ltd
Maps by Tim Smith

First published 1977 by Holmes McDougall Ltd, Edinburgh

This edition 1992 by
CollinsEducational
77-85 Fulham Palace Road
Hammersmith London W6 8JB

Reprinted 1993, 1995

ISBN 0003271129

Project team

David Sylvester (Director to 1975)
Tony Boddington (Director from 1975)
Gwenifer Griffiths (1975-1976)
William Harrison (1972-1975)
John Mann (1974-1975)
Aileen Plummer (from 1972)
Denis Shemilt (Evaluator from 1974)
Peter Wenham (1972-1974)

Acknowledgements

The Project team would like to thank the following
trial school teachers for their help in preparing
sections of this book:

B. Bainbridge *Summerhill School, Kingswinford,
West Midlands*
A. Dunphy *Ellowes Hall School, Lower Gornal,
Dudley, West Midlands*
T. H. Rowland *Blyth Tynedale High School,
Blyth, Northumberland*
J. Scott *Glossop School, Glossop, Derbyshire*
and J. B. Davies *Postgraduate student, School of
History, Leeds University*

Printed in Great Britain
by Scotprint Ltd, Musselburgh

Schools Council
History 13-16 Project

Enquiry in depth

The American West 1840-95

Acknowledgements

The authors and publishers are grateful to the following for permission to reproduce copyright material:

Photographs and illustrations

Front cover *Fort Laramie*, The Beinecke Rare Book and Manuscript Library, Yale University, USA; page 8 *'A land of cows and sky'*, facing p. 118 in Richard Irving Dodge, *The Hunting Grounds of the Great West*, 1877; page 9 *Cacti in the desert*, p. 256 in J. P. Dunn, *Massacre of the Mountains*, 1886; page 12 *The Canon de Chelley*, The Librarian, Exeter University Library (original photograph by Edward Curtis, print by John Webb FRPS), *Hunting buffalo on foot*, The Mansell Collection; page 14 *A buffalo hunt*, p. 138 in Dodge, *Hunting Grounds*; page 15 *A Mandan chief by George Catlin*, The Mansell Collection; page 16 *Plains Indian signalling*, Western Americana Picture Library, *A Sioux Village*, Mansell Collection; page 17 *Moving camp by Catlin*, Mansell Collection, *Inside a tepee*, West Point Museum, New York; page 18 *Indian council*, p. 265, Dodge, *Hunting Grounds*; page 19 *Grand chief of the Pawnees*, p. 372, Dodge, *Hunting Grounds*; page 20 *Bison hunt*, Mansell Collection; page 21 *Young brave outside tepee*, Radio Times Hulton Picture Library; page 22 *Young Cheyenne girl*, The Librarian, Exeter University Library (Edward Curtis original); page 23 *Indian art*, plate 232 in George Catlin, *Letters and Notes on the Manners, Customs and Conditions of the North American Indians*, Vol. 2, 1841; page 24 *A Comanche trick of war by* Remington Western Americana Picture Library, *An Indian horse race*, Mansell Collection; page 25 *Colonel Dodge meets a Comanche war party*, plate 151, Catlin Vol 2; page 26 *Indian scalping dead enemy*, Mansell Collection; page 27 *Scalp dance*, facing p. 278, Dodge, *Hunting Grounds*; page 28 *Indian weapons and medicine bags*, plate 18, Catlin Vol 1; page 29 *Blackfoot medicine man*, Mansell Collection; page 30 *Buffalo dance*, *Harper's Weekly*, 7 May 1887; page 31 *The sun dancer*, The Librarian, Exeter University Library (Edward Curtis original); page 32 *Sun Dance Lodge by Edward Curtis*, Boston Public Library, USA; page 33 *Medicine wheel*, Western History Research Center, University of Wyoming, *Arapaho pouch*, American Museum of Natural History, New York; page 34 *Medicine Bluff Creek*, Smithsonian Institution, National Anthropological Archives, Washington DC; page 35 *'Okolohama'*, facing p. 290, Dodge, *Hunting Grounds*; page 36 *Miners in gold rush*, Western Americana Picture Library; page 39 *Wagon train to Oregon*, Mary Evans Picture Library; page 41 *Virginia City*, Western Americana Picture Library; page 42 *Brigham Young and Salt Lake City*, Mary Evans Picture Library, *Joseph Smith's first vision*, p. 1 in T. B. H. Stenhouse. *The Rocky Mountain Saints*, London 1874; pages 43 to 47 in Stenhouse, *Rocky Mountain Saints*; page 47 *A first view of polygamy*, Mary Evans Picture Library; page 48 *Brigham Young*, Mansell Collection; page 50 *Exodus from Nauvoo*, Mary Evans Picture Library; page 51 *On the march*, p. 251 in Stenhouse, *A Mormon camp*, Mary Evans Library; page 52 *Along the route*, p. 335, Stenhouse, *First view of the Great Salt Lake*, Mansell Collection; page 54 *Salt Lake City in 1873*, Mary Evans Library; page 55 *Temple, Tabernacle and Assembly Hall*, Mansell Collection; page 56 *Pioneer Mill*, p. 722, Stenhouse; page 57 *Hand cart emigrants*, p. 310, Stenhouse, *'Uncle Sam's Abscess'*, from William Jarman's tract (same title) 1884; page 58 *US troops*, Stenhouse; page 59 *Brigham Young on his travels*, Stenhouse, *Cartoon of Young's widows*, Mansell Collection; page 61 *Longhorn cattle*, Western Americana Picture Library; page 62 *Spanish vaqueros*, Mary Evans Library; page 63 *Roping a Longhorn*, Western Americana Library; page 64 *Charles Goodnight*, Western Americana Library, *On the Long Drive*, *Harper's Weekly*, 2 May 1874; page 67 *Cattle train leaving Ellsworth, Kansas*, Western Americana Library, *Loading at Wichita*, p. 284 in J. G. McCoy, *Historic Sketches of Cattle Trade*, 1874, *Union Stockyards*, Chicago, *Harper's Weekly*, 31 October 1868; page 69 *John Illiffe*, Western Americana Library; page 70 *Union Pacific construction workers*, Mary Evans Library, *John W. Snyder*, Western Americana Library; page 71 *Ranchhouse in Wyoming*, Western Americana Library; page 73 *Negro cowboy* and page 74 *Trail boss*, Western Americana Library; page 75 *Cowboys at a line camp*, reproduced by permission of The British Library Board, from Theodore Roosevelt, *F. Remington, Ranch Life and the Hunting Trail*, 1888, *Bringing in a downer*, p. 219 in Ramon Adams, *Old Time Cowhand*, Macmillan, New York 1961; page 76 *Pulling a cow out of mud*, The British Library Board (p. 17 Roosevelt); page 77 *The round-up*, Mary Evans Library, *Branding*, Western Americana Library; page 78 *Brands of the XIT ranch*, The University of Oklahoma Press; page 79 *Cowboys eating*, The British Library Board (p. 5 Roosevelt); page 80 *A Prairie grave*, p. 325 in C. Neider, *The Great West*, Bonanza Books New York 1958; page 81 *A Stampede*, The British Library Board (p. 69, Roosevelt); page 82 *An Abilene dance house*, p. 140, McCoy, *A cowboy in the rain*, Mansall Collection; page 83 *Cattle in a blizzard*, *Harper's Weekly*, 27 February 1886, *Granville Stuart*, Montana Historical Society, Helena, USA; page 84 *Waiting for the chinook*, Western Americana Library; page 85 *The first poster advertising barbed wire, 1874*, Carl S. Dentzel Collection, Southwest Museum, Los Angeles, Ca. USA, *Riding the fence*, p. 205, Adams; page 86 *Peter M. Barnes and family*, Solomon D. Butcher Collection, Nebraska State Historical Society; page 90 *Emigrants moving* and *Former slaves*, Solomon D. Butcher Collection; page 91 *The City of Babylon*, Richardson, *Beyond the Mississippi*, American Publishing Company, 1867; page 92 *Dishonest land claims*, Solomon D. Butcher Collection; page 93 *Gathering pumpkins*, Mansell Collection; page 95 *Swedish immigrants to Kansas*, Kansas State Historical Society, Topeka, USA; page 96 *An emigrant train*, *Harper's Weekly*, 13 November 1886, *Railroad company land advert*, Baker Library, Harvard University; page 97 *The first season*, *Harper's Weekly*, 24 January, 1874; pages 99 to 101, Solomon D. Butcher Collection, Nebraska State Historical Society; page 103 *Breaking the soil*, *Harper's Weekly*, 9 May 1868; page 104 *Harvesting*, Western Americana Library, *Threshing*, Mansell Collection; page 105 *Winnowing*, Mansell Collection; page 106 *'Drouthy Kansas'* by Henry Worrall, Kansas State Historical Society, *Fighting a prairie fire*, *Harper's Weekly*, 28 February 1874; page 107 *Grasshoppers stopping a train*, Solomon D. Butcher Collection; page 109 *'The farmer's life. . .'* Mary Evans Library; page 110 *Windpump*, Solomon D. Butcher Collection, *Steam powered threshing*, Mary Evans Library; page 111 *Arrival of grain in New York, 1877*, Library of Congress, Washington DC, USA; page 112 *Plains Indians* by Edward Curtis, The Librarian, Exeter University Library; page 116 *'The trail of tears'* by Robert Lindneux, Western Americana Library; page 117 *Indian hunter ordering wagons to retreat*, *Harper's Weekly*, 19 September 1874; page 119 *Fort Laramie* (as cover); page 120 *Night attack*, p. 380, Dodge; page 122 *Miners in Colorado gold rush 1859*, *Harper's Weekly*, 14 October 1876; page 123 *Recruiting poster*, Library, The State Historical Society of Colorado Denver, USA; page 124 *Colonel Chivington* and *Attack at dawn*, Western Americana Library; page 125 *Indians attack stage coach*, Mansell Collection; page 126 *General Sherman*, *Harper's Weekly*, 17 December 1864; page 127 *Peace Commission*, p. 270, Dodge; page 128 *Ten Bears, Comanche chief*, Western Americana Library; page 129 *Indians attack navvies*, Mansell Collection; page 130 *Chief Gall of the Hunkpapa Sioux*, Smithsonian Institution, Washington DC, *Charles Goodnight's ranch*, p. 284, McCoy; page 131 *Custer*, Mary Evans Library; page 132 *Battle of the Washita*, courtesy of the Everett D. Graff Collection, The Newberry Library, Chicago, USA; page 133 *Buffalo hunters*, Western Americana Library; page 135 *Ration day at Pine Ridge*, Western Americana Library; page 136 *Apaches in Arizona*, The Librarian, Exeter University Library; page 137 *An agency policeman by Remington*, The British Library Board (p. 130, Roosevelt); page 139 *Indian ploughing by Remington*, Mansell Collection; page 140 *'Custer's last stand'* by *Kurz and Allison*, Culver Pictures Inc, New York, *Headlines from 'New York Herald'*, *New York Herald*, 6 July 1876; page 142 *Black Elk*, John G. Neihardt Trust, Columbia, Mo., USA, *Fetterman Massacre*, *Harper's Weekly*, 23 March 1867; page 143 *Red Cloud of the Oglala Sioux*, Courtesy of Museum of the American Indian, Heye Foundation, New York; page 144 *Death of the mail carrier, by Sitting Bull*, Mansell Collection, *Custer*, Mary Evans Library; page 145 *Custer in the Black Hills*, US Signal Corps, photo no. 111-SC-98512, National Archives, Washington DC, *Mining town, Deadwood*, *Harper's Weekly*, 28 October 1876; page 146 *Sitting Bull of the Hunkpapa Sioux*, *General Philip Sheridan*, in J. P. Dunn, *Massacre of the Mountains*; page 148 *Sioux scouts*, Mary Evans Library; page 151 *'Custer's last stand' by Paxson*, Western Americana Library; page 152 *Custer on an outing*, US Signal Corps, photo no. 111-SC-83991, National Archives; page 153 *General Terry*, *Harper's Weekly*, 4 February 1865; page 154 *Custer's Crow scouts*, Boston Public Library, Boston Mass, USA, *Fighting the Sioux*, Mary Evans Library; page 155 *Winchester magazine rifle*, Western Americana Library, *Cartoon*, *Harper's Weekly*, 5 August 1876; page 156 *Crook's expedition*, US War Dept, General Staff 165-FF-3C-12, National Archives, *Indian campaign*, *Custer's prisoners*, *Harper's Weekly*, 26 December 1868; page 157 *Crazy Horse*, Western Americana Library; page 158 *Woodgatherers*, Smithsonian Institution, Washington, *Slaughter of buffalo*, p. 14, Dodge; page 159 *Ghost dance*, The British Library Board (p. 58 in Hamlyn Garland, *Book of the North American Indian*), *Frozen body of Chief*, Western Americana Library; page 160 *George Ruffner*, Arizona Historical Society; page 163 *Joe Cheesman*, Oklahoma Historical Society; page 165 *Creede, Colorado*, Western Americana Library, *Gold and silver mining*, *Harper's Weekly*, 18 July 1874; page 166 *Wells Fargo notice*, Wells Fargo Bank History Room, San Francisco Ca., USA; pages 167 to 169 Western Americana Library; page 170 *Vigilantes*, *Harper's Weekly*, 11 April 1876; page 171 *Double hanging*, Denver Public Library, Western History Dept., *Virginia City*, Mary Evans Library; page 172 *Helena Jail, Montana*, Montana Historical Society, *California's first jail, Monterey*, Mercaldo Archives; page 173 *robbers in coffins*, Denver Public Library, Western History Dept.; page 174 *Judge Roy Bean*, Western History Collection, University of Oklahoma Library; page 175 *Tombstone's court*, Arizona Historical Society; page 176 *Vigilante hangings*, The California Historical Society, *Cattle rustlers on the Texas border*, *Harper's Weekly*, 1 January 1874; page 177 *Wire cutting in Nebraska*, Solomon D. Butcher Collection, *Cattle barons*, Western History Research Center, University of Wyoming Laramie, USA; page 178 *Montana cattlemen*, Montana Historical Society, *Cattle Kate*, Western Americana Library; page 179 *Wyoming stockmen and Texas gunmen*, Western History Research Center, University of Wyoming, *Sheriff Frank Canton*, Western History Collections, University of Oklahoma Library; page 181 *Sheriff Red Angus*, Wyoming State Archives and Historical Dept., Cheyenne, USA; page 182 *Fort McKinney*, Western History Research Center, University of Wyoming, *'What an unbranded cow has cost'*, Mary Evans Picture Library.

Extracts

Source material acknowledgements appear at the end of each extract. Where several extracts are from the same source, the acknowledgement is given in full at the end of the first extract to appear. Also Sources 63, 64, 65, 66 reprinted by permission of the Colorado Associated University Press; sources 79, 80, 87, 88, 90, 91, 93, by permission of the University of Nebraska Press; sources 14, 32, 33, 125, 128, 130, 140, 142 by permission of the John G. Neihardt Trust and Barrie & Jenkins Ltd; source 75 by permission of the Swallow Press, Inc, Chicago; sources 72, 74, 117, 120, 122, 151, 161 by permission of the University of Oklahoma Press, Norman, Oklahoma, sources 81, 85, 94, 131, 138 by permission of The Lakeside Press, R. R. Donnelly & Sons Co., Chicago.

A Who's Who? of famous artists of the American West

George Catlin 1796-1872

Catlin was born in Pennsylvania, USA in 1796. He abandoned his law studies in 1823 to take up portrait painting, which he taught himself. Because of a life-long interest in Indian culture, in 1829 Catlin began a series of visits to various tribes, mainly on the Great Plains. As a result of his eight years in the West, he made over 500 paintings and sketches which were exhibited in Europe and America between 1837 and 1845.

Robert Lindneux 1871-1970

Lindneux was born in New York City and studied art in Germany and France before returning to the USA in 1893. He then settled in Colorado and became interested in western history. He was a friend of Charles M. Russell and 'Buffalo Bill' Cody.

Alfred Jacob Miller 1810-1874

Miller was born in Maryland and studied art in the USA and in Paris. In 1837 he accompanied a hunting excursion in the West. As a result of this experience he produced many studies of mountain scenery, and the lives of Indians and fur trappers.

Frederic Remington 1861-1909

Remington was born in New York State and studied at Yale Art School. In 1880, for health reasons, he began travelling in the West. Soon Remington began producing western sketches for magazines such as *Harper's Weekly*. He became famous as an accurate observer and reporter of Indians, cowboys, soldiers and horses. During the last twenty years of his life he produced 2700 paintings and drawings and 24 bronze sculptures.

Charles Marion Russell 1864-1926

Russell was born in St Louis and spent his youth as a ranch hand and manager in Montana. It was at this time that he first began to sketch scenes showing Indians and cowboys. In the following years he produced a great volume of paintings and sketches about western life.

Charles Schreyvogel 1861-1912

Schreyvogel was born in New York City and studied art in Germany. In 1893 he travelled West for his health and first became interested in military life. In the following years he produced 'action' paintings of the soldiers' life on the Plains in the 1860s, 1870s and 1880s. He died of accidental blood poisoning in 1912.

Contents

Introduction

This is a study of the American West between the years 1840 and 1895, and the actions, beliefs and attitudes of some of the people who lived there. But first, what do we mean by 'The American West' —where is it and what was it like?

The idea of 'The West'

Throughout American History the term 'The West' has meant different things to different people. In the early days of the seventeenth century, when the first colonists were still scattered along the Atlantic seaboard, 'The West' began only a few kilometres inland. By 1800, however, as more settlers came to America from Europe, the frontier (the line which divided the inhabited lands of the East from the uninhabited lands of the West) had moved inland as far as the Appalachian Mountains. By the time that this study begins, settlers had moved across the mountains as far as the Mississippi River. So, for us, 'The American West' can be said to be all that land which lies west- wards from the Mississippi to the Pacific coast, bounded by the Canadian border in the north and the Mexican border in the south.

A strange land

In 1840 a few settlers had ventured across the Mississippi River and established farms on its west bank as well as in Texas. There were also a few hunters and trappers wandering in the mountains and small groups of Spanish and British colonists in New Mexico, California and Oregon.

Nevertheless the only inhabitants of the greater part of this vast area were animals, birds and the native peoples of America, the Indians.

As a result of the reports of hunters, trappers and explorers, it was already clear to eastern settlers that 'The West' was not only bigger than they had ever imagined, but it was also a strange land—different by

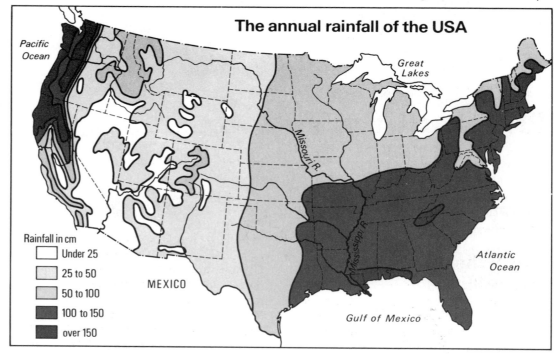

The annual rainfall of the USA

Pacific Ocean

Great Lakes

Missouri R.

Mississippi R.

Rainfall in cm
- Under 25
- 25 to 50
- 50 to 100
- 100 to 150
- over 150

MEXICO

Atlantic Ocean

Gulf of Mexico

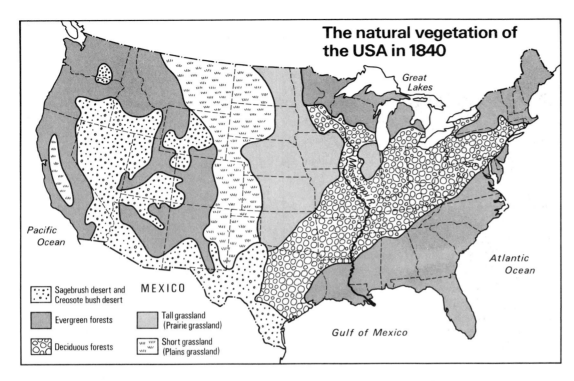

The natural vegetation of the USA in 1840

Legend:
- Sagebrush desert and Creosote bush desert
- Evergreen forests
- Deciduous forests
- Tall grassland (Prairie grassland)
- Short grassland (Plains grassland)

Great Lakes

Pacific Ocean

Atlantic Ocean

MEXICO

Gulf of Mexico

far from their familiar well wooded and well watered farmlands. Moreover, it was an area of great contrasts: not one region but many, each differing from the other in geography, climate, vegetation and wild life.

From the Pacific to the mountains

In the far west were the Pacific coastlands of California and Oregon. In the valleys to the south with their grassland and good soil, the climate was dry and sunny. In the northern valleys the climate was mild and wet and there were thick forests.

To the east of the Pacific coastlands and stretching the whole length of the continent was a vast region of mountains and plateaux. This formed a great barrier between the valleys of California and Oregon, and the rest of America. The Sierra Nevada was the first range of mountains; a towering wall of peaks from 3500 to 4500 metres high. In northern California these merged into the Cascades, a chain of mountains 100-130 kilometres wide. Both the Cascades and the Sierra Nevada had heavy rainfall and were thickly forested.

The plateaux region

Beyond these mountain ranges was the plateaux region. The Columbia Plateau lay to the north; an area with rich volcanic soil but little rainfall, hence its semi-desert vegetation, the sage brush. Below this area was a depression known as the Great Basin. Here low-lying mountains were interspersed with desert-like valleys. Westerly winds from the Sierra Nevada swept over the Great Basin. These winds were so dry that they actually picked up the remaining moisture from the parched soil. Sage brush covered the northern part of the Basin. In this area lay the Great Salt Lake. The southern half was mainly desert land with a rainfall of 5 cm a year. Here only cacti and creosote bushes survived.

South of the Great Basin was the Colorado River Plateau which ranged between 1500 and 3350 m above sea level. Today, this is still a land of ravines and canyons, of sage brush, cacti and alkali dust.

The Rocky Mountains

The Rockies formed the eastern edge of the mountain and plateaux region. This giant mountain chain with its towering peaks stretched along the backbone of the continent, interrupted only by the Wyoming

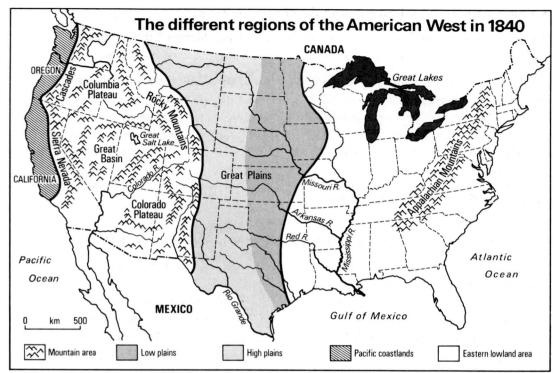

The different regions of the American West in 1840

CANADA
OREGON
Cascades
Columbia Plateau
Rocky Mountains
Great Lakes
Sierra Nevada
Great Salt Lake
Great Basin
Colorado R.
CALIFORNIA
Great Plains
Missouri R.
Colorado Plateau
Appalachian Mountains
Arkansas R.
Red R.
Pacific Ocean
Mississippi R.
Atlantic Ocean
Rio Grande
MEXICO
Gulf of Mexico

0 km 500

Mountain area | Low plains | High plains | Pacific coastlands | Eastern lowland area

ot temperature. The most constant weather feature of the plains, however, is the ferocious wind which blows all year round. It was this wind which led many travellers to call the waving prairies, 'the seas of grass' and their covered wagons, 'prairie schooners'. In the summer, the wind was scorching hot, drying up the land and the alkaline waters of the river. In the winter the 'Northers' brought blizzards, tornadoes and hailstorms. In spring the warm 'Chinook' blew down from the Rockies melting the snows with amazing speed. Despite these extremes of climate, the Great Plains had many wild animals—all of them creatures who had adapted well to their environment: antelopes, prairie dogs, jack rabbits, gophers and above all, huge herds of bison (or buffalo, as they are often called).

Basin. On the lower slopes grew forests of pine, spruce and fir trees. In 1840 these forests were the territory of wolves, grizzly bears, mountain lions, beavers and the handful of men who hunted them.

The Great Plains

Finally, from the foothills of the Rockies to the Mississippi stretched the Great Plains with their gently rolling grassland and slow flowing rivers. Near the Rockies the grass was short and tough but towards the Mississippi it became tall 'prairie' grass.

Trees were few and far between, growing mainly near the rivers. Only in a few areas did the scenery vary. In the north, around the Black Hills of Dakota (one of the few wooded areas) were the 'Badlands'; a region of soft rock which has been eroded by wind and rain into fantastic shapes. In the south the plains became more arid and here the vegetation was of the semi-desert type: mesquite grass, black chaparral and prickly pear.

No other part of America had such unpredictable weather or such extremes

ABOVE RIGHT: Cacti in the desert
ABOVE: The Great Plains: a land of 'cows and sky'

The myth of 'The Great American Desert'

Of all the regions of the West, the white hunters, explorers and settlers found the Great Plains most forbidding. From the time that they were first explored in the early 1540s, the plains came to be known as a land of nothing but 'cows and sky,' 'The Great American Desert'. Between 1540 and 1840 all the scientists, soldiers and explorers who ventured into the plains returned with the same belief—that this was a land fit only for Indians and buffalo (sources 1-3). Nevertheless it is the Great Plains which we shall be studying in the greatest detail. We shall look first at the people who lived there before the white Americans, the Plains Indians. Then we shall look at the early settlers who shunned the plains, crossing them only out of necessity in search of land or gold on the west coast. Finally we shall consider the people who at last learned how to live in this land: miners, cattlemen, farmers and soldiers—the white settlers who fought to take it from its first inhabitants, the Indians.

SOURCE 1 Coronado's description of the Great Plains, 1540-2

Coronado was a Spanish explorer who set off north from Mexico City in 1540 in search of gold. He found no gold, but left us this description of what he did see:

> The country they [the buffalo] travelled over was so level and smooth that if one looked at them the sky could be seen between their legs. . . . The country was so level that men became lost when they went off half a league. . . . It would not be possible to establish a settlement here . . . the winter could not possibly be spent here, because there is no wood, nor cloth with which to protect the men except the skins which the natives wear . . .

George Parker Winship (trans), *The Coronado Expedition 1540-1542*, 14th Annual Report of the Bureau of American Ethnology, Part I, p. 543, [US] Government Printing Office, 1896

SOURCE 2 Major Stephen Long's description of the Great Plains, 1819-20

Major Long led an expedition into the Great Plains. After describing the wild life of the plains he made the following comments:

> In regard to this extensive section of country, I do not hesitate in giving the opinion, that it is almost wholly unfit for cultivation, and of course uninhabitable by a people depending upon agriculture for their subsistence. Although tracts of fertile land considerably extensive are occasionally to be met with, yet the scarcity of wood and water, will prove an insuperable obstacle in the way of settling the country.

Early Western Travel Series, Vol. XVII, Arthur H. Clark Company, 1904-7, pp. 147-8

SOURCE 3 Colonel Richard Irving Dodge's comments on the Plains, 1877

> When I was a schoolboy, my map of the United States showed between the Missouri River and the Rocky Mountains a long and broad white blotch, upon which was printed in small capitals THE GREAT AMERICAN DESERT—UNEXPLORED. What was then 'unexplored' is now almost thoroughly known. What then was regarded as a desert supports, in some [areas], thriving populations. The blotch of thirty years ago is now known as THE PLAINS.

Richard Irving Dodge, *The Hunting Grounds of the Great West*, Chatto and Windus, 1877, p. 3

1
The Plains Indians: their life and culture

The first Americans

Long before the Europeans discovered America, Indians inhabited the continent. The first Indians are thought to have emigrated from Siberia to Alaska somewhere between 10 000 and 40 000 years ago. They may have been hunters who crossed the frozen Bering Strait in search of food. They found a new land with plenty of game and decided to stay. As more Indians came across the Strait, groups gradually made their way south and east.

Over many thousands of years they spread over the whole of North and Central America and even into South America. In time, the Indians formed themselves into many different tribal groups. Each group developed its own particular way of life which fitted the geography, climate and vegetation of its

OPPOSITE: A warrior band

own area (see map, p. 13). Although there were many different cultural groups amongst the Indians, we shall be studying only one of these in detail: the Plains Indians.

Before the eighteenth century most tribes lived in the fertile agricultural or forest regions of the east and west coasts, or in the area near the Great Lakes. Few Indians actually lived out on the 'High Plains'. Some tribes built semi-permanent villages on the edges of the plains. These Prairie Indians erected lodges of earth or bark and raised crops of maize, pumpkins and beans. They also supplemented their diet with buffalo meat. But it was not easy to hunt the buffalo: before the arrival of the Europeans, there were no horses in America, and so the Prairie Indians had to stalk their prey on foot.

During the summer months the Indians would load their possessions on to a dog-

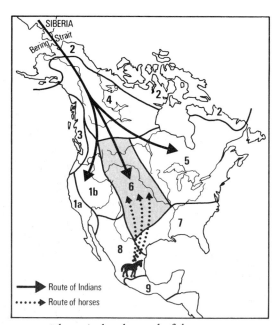

ABOVE: The arrival and spread of the Indians and the horse in North America

ABOVE: The Canon de Chelley

BELOW: Indians dressed in wolf skins stalking buffalo on foot by George Catlin, 1841

drag and follow the buffalo. But all too often, the Indians found that they could not keep up with the herds. So despite their skill with bow, arrow and lance, there was not enough meat to eat for much of the year.

The coming of the horse

Then came the horse and the whole way of life of the Prairie Indians changed. It was the Spanish conquerors of New Mexico who introduced horses into North America in the 1590s. Gradually, by trade and theft, the Indians acquired some of these horses. In addition many horses escaped from Spanish ranches and missions and migrated northwards. By 1700 herds of wild horses were wandering on the plains.

One by one the tribes learned that the horse was a better form of transport than the dog. A horse-drag could carry four times the load of a dog and take it twice as far each day. In time, the tribes mastered the art of riding and found a new way of life.

Many tribes abandoned their semi-permanent villages and their maize patches for ever to become full-time hunters. At this time, more Indians from the eastern woodlands also began to move onto the plains. They were being driven west by white men. From the grasslands, river valleys and mountains bordering the plains came the Cheyennes, Sioux, Comanches, Crows and the Arapahos. These Indians became truly nomadic tribes, living on the plains and depending entirely on the buffalo for their food and shelter. Some tribes, like the Pawnees, the Mandans and the Hidatsa, continued to live in more permanent villages on the east of the plains during the winter. Each summer they too left their earth lodges and went in search of the buffalo. As a result of the coming of the horse, the whole way of life of many of the Prairie Indian tribes came to revolve around the seasonal coming and going of the buffalo. They became the Plains Indians.

The Plains Indians and the Whiteman

'I find the principal cause why we underrate and despise the savage is generally because we do not understand him.' These are the words of George Catlin, an

American painter who explored the West in the 1830s. After visiting many of the tribes he came both to know and to admire the Indians (source 4). In 1840, however, many white men were still far from understanding the Indians and their way of life. This was partly because many white men had never met any Indians. Even more, it was because most American settlers judged the Indians according to white men's ideas and beliefs. Looked at in this way the Indians seemed to them little more than superstitious and uncivilised savages (source 5).

In fact, given the problems they had to face, the Plains Indians had found, as Catlin realised, an 'ingenious way to live'. The environment of the Great Plains was a hostile one, different from that of the East where the whiteman lived. The weapons and tools of the Plains Indians were simple—stone knives and scrapers, bone awls, bows and arrows. Unlike the white man with 'modern' technology and inventions at his disposal, the Indians were unable to change their environment to fit their way of life. Instead, they had to make a way of life which fitted in with their environment. As a result, they developed ideas and customs, values and attitudes to life which were very different from those of white Americans.

The Plains Indian tribes and their hunting grounds in 1840

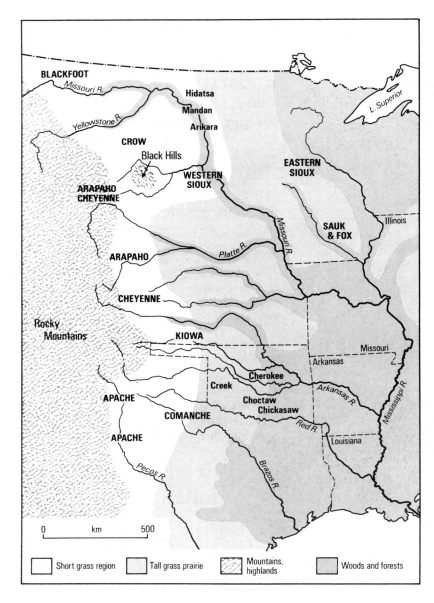

SOURCE 4 The Indians as human beings

From what I have seen of these people I say that there is nothing very strange in their character. It is a simple one, and easy to be understood if the right means be taken to familiarise ourselves with it. The North American Indian in his native state is an honest, faithful, brave, warlike, cruel, revengeful, relentless—yet honourable, contemplative and religious being. From the very many acts of their hospitality and kindness, I pronounce them, by nature, a kind and hospitable people.

George Catlin, *Letters and Notes on the Manners, Customs and Condition of the North American Indians*, Wiley & Putnam (New York), 1841, Vol. I

SOURCE 5 The Indian as a savage and enemy described by Horace Greeley, a contemporary journalist

The Indians are children. Their wars, treaties, habitations, crafts, comforts, all belong to the very lowest ages of human existence. Squalid and conceited, proud and worthless, lazy and lousy, they will strut out or drink out their miserable existence, and at length afford the world relief by dying out of it.

Horace Greeley, *An Overland Journey from New York to San Francisco in the Summer of 1859*, Alfred A. Knopf, 1964, pp. 119, 121

BELOW: A buffalo hunt

The Plains Indians in 1840
Food, clothing and shelter
The basic needs of the Indians (as for all people) were for food, clothing and shelter. The buffalo provided the answer to these needs and the horse enabled the Indians to hunt the buffalo effectively. The buffalo hunt, therefore, became the most important activity for all the Plains tribes (source 6). After the hunt the Indians would feast on the fresh buffalo meat. Most of the meat, however, had to be dried and preserved for use during the long winter months, for then the herds moved south and fresh meat was hard to find. The hides and sinews of the buffalo

were also carefully dressed and preserved.
These provided the raw material for the
Indians' home—the tepee—their clothes and
many other items of everyday use
(source 7).

SOURCE 6 How buffalo meat and hides were preserved and used

The Blackfeet, Crows, Sioux and Assinneboins, have lodges of buffalo skins sewed together and made into the form of a tent. The Crows make the most beautiful lodge. They dress the skins as white as linen, and beautifully garnish them with porcupine quills. They dry the buffalo meat, making pemmican, and preserving the marrow fat for winter.

The Crows, like the Blackfeet, are beautifully costumed, the skins are delicately and whitely dressed. The Crows surpass the civilised world in the beauty of their skin-dressing. The art of tanning is unknown to them. The usual mode of dressing the buffalo, and other skins, is by immersing them for a few days under a lye from ashes and water, until the hair can be removed. Then they are strained upon a frame or upon the ground. There they remain for several days, with the brains of the buffalo or elk spread over them; and at last finished by 'graining' by the squaws. They use the shoulder-blade of the animal sharpened at the edge; and they scrape the fleshy side of the skin thereby drying and softening the skin. The greater part of these skins, however, go through the process of smoking.

Catlin, *Manners, Customs and Conditions of the North American Indian*, Vol. I, pp. 43-5

SOURCE 7 An explorer of the Great Plains in 1846 describes the uses of the buffalo to the Indian

The buffalo supplies them [the Indians] with the necessaries of life; with habitations, food, clothing, beds and fuel, strings for their bows, glue, thread, cordage, trail ropes for their horses, covering for their saddles, vessels to hold water, boats to cross streams, and the means of purchasing all they want from the traders. When the buffalo are extinct, they too must dwindle away.

Francis Parkman, *The Oregon Trail*, Lancer Books Inc, 1968, pp. 176-7

BELOW: A Mandan chief in his decorated buffalo robes: a drawing by George Catlin

ABOVE: A Plains Indian signalling with a buffalo robe by Frederic Remington. The Indians devised other methods of sending messages over long distances using smoke and hand signals

BELOW: A Sioux village by George Catlin

The life of a wanderer

Since the Indians depended entirely on the buffalo for the necessities of life, they had to adapt the pattern of their lives to the movement of the buffalo. During the summer months the tribes moved constantly, following the buffalo herds as they grazed on the plains grasslands. Only in winter did the Indians settle in one place for any length of time. Then it was out of necessity—to protect themselves against the bitter cold of the snow and wind.

The tepee

Because of their nomadic life the Indians had to have a home which was easy to build, quick to take down, and light to carry. It also had to give protection against the changeable weather on the plains. The Indians had a simple and effective answer to this problem: the buffalo skin tepee. This was an ideal portable home and the horse-drag an excellent means of transport (source 8).

Nomadic Indians had few personal possessions and Indian women became ingenious at storing away food and clothing in a small space. For this they used rawhide bags called parflèches. These could be hung from the poles of the tepee in camp or across the horse's back when travelling (sources 9, 10).

SOURCE 8 Moving camp

Their lodges are taken down in a few minutes by the squaws and easily transported to any part of the country where they wish to encamp. They generally move six or eight times in the summer, following the immense herds of buffaloes. The manner in which an encampment of Indians strike their tents and transport them is curious. I saw an encampment of Sioux, consisting of six hundred lodges, struck, and all things packed and on the move in a very few minutes. The chief sends his runners through the village a few hours before they are to start, announcing his determination to move, and the hour fixed upon. At the time announced, the lodge of the chief is seen flapping in the wind, a part of the poles having been taken out from under it; this is the signal, and in one minute, six hundred of them all were flat upon the ground.

Catlin, *Manners, Customs and Condition of the North American Indians*, Vol. I, pp. 43-4

SOURCE 9 Inside an Indian tepee, described by Colonel Dodge, 1877

The home or lodge of the Plains Indians is from twelve to twenty feet [4-6 m] in diameter, and about fifteen feet [4.5 m] high. The fire is built in the centre, and the smoke escapes through an aperture at the top. The draught is, however, very defective, and the lodge is usually in cold weather, too full of smoke to be bearable to anyone but an Indian. It is, however, admirably adapted to their necessities. Its shape secures it from the danger of being over-turned by windstorms, and with very little fuel it can be kept warm and comfortable even in the coldest weather.

The beds are piles of buffalo robes and blankets, spread on the ground as close to the outer circumference as possible. They serve as sleeping places by night, and seats by day. In this small space are often crowded eight or ten persons, possibly of three or four different families. Since the cooking, eating, living and sleeping are all done in the one room, it soon becomes inconceivably filthy.

The wealth of the Indian is in his horse and mules. He has no desire for more things than are necessary for the wants of his family for the time being.

Dodge, *Hunting Grounds of the Great West*, p. 311

SOURCE 10 'The tepee is much better to live in', a comment by Chief Flying Hawk of the Oglala Sioux (1852-1931)

The tepee is much better to live in; always clean, warm in winter, cool in summer; easy to move. The white man builds big house, cost much money, like big cage, shut out sun, can never move. Indians and animals know better how to live than white men; nobody can be in good health if he does not have all the time fresh air, sunshine and good water. If the Great Spirit wanted men to stay in one place he would make the world stand still; but He made it always to change, so birds and animals can move and always have green grass and ripe berries. The white man does not obey the Great Spirit; that is why the Indians never could agree with him.

M. I. McCreight, *Firewater and Forked Tongues: A Sioux Chief Interprets U.S. History*, Trail's End Publishing Co, 1947, p. 61

TOP: Moving camp by George Catlin
ABOVE: Inside an Indian tepee by
Peter Rindisbacher, 1806-1834

The chief, the tribe and the band

The Plains Indians needed to find sufficient grass for their horses and meat for their families, so they spent most of the year travelling in small groups or bands. The Cheyenne tribe, for example, had ten major bands. Each band had between three and five hundred people under a chief who was a respected warrior. Some tribes, such as the Sioux and the Cheyenne, had two

ABOVE: Peace or war? An Indian council

kinds of chief: one for wartime and one for peace.

A council of elders usually governed each band. They would meet with the chief to discuss important matters and make decisions. Societies of warriors, often known as 'dog soldiers', enforced the council's decisions and organised much of the day to day life of the band (source 11).

Most of the year, the bands of each tribe travelled independently. Only in the summer, when the buffalo were plentiful and the grass lush, did all the bands from some tribes meet together. Then, tribes like the Cheyenne set up vast summer camps and held special ceremonies. The summer camp was often the one occasion when the tribal council of all the chiefs met. The Cheyenne sent four chiefs from each band to their tribal council and, in addition, chose four outstanding men to be overall chiefs of the whole tribe. In the council meetings, the chiefs discussed issues affecting the whole tribe, especially questions of peace or war.

The feasts, ceremonies and meetings held during the summer helped to draw the different bands closer together and remind them of their tribal loyalties. Even so, the bands of a tribe often failed to agree to act together. Frequently some bands would be at peace while others went on the warpath. Many white Americans, with their own ideas about government, found it difficult to understand the limited powers of the chiefs or the loose grouping of bands in a tribe (source 12). The independence of the bands presented problems later for the US government when they tried to make binding treaties for the whole tribe. White Americans reached the view that the Plains Indians were 'without government'. Few realised that the Indians had a system of government, which although different from that of white Americans, was, nevertheless, well adapted to their way of life (source 13).

SOURCE 11 The role of the Dog Soldiers, by Colonel Dodge, 1877

Whatever the power of the chief and council there is another power to which both have to yield. This power is the hunters of the tribe, who form a sort of guild. Among the Cheyennes these men are called 'dog soldiers'. This 'guild' comprises the whole working force of the band. It is they who protect and supply the women and children. From them come all orders for marches. By them the encampments are selected. They supply the guards for the camp and designate the hunting parties.

One of the most important functions of the 'dog soldiers' is the protection of the game. Except when laying in the supply of meat for winter, only sufficient buffalo is killed for the current supply of the camp. Great care is taken not to alarm the herds, which will feed for days in the vicinity of an Indian camp of a thousand souls, while a half a dozen white men would have driven them all away in a day.

Dodge, *Hunting Grounds of the Great West*, pp. 266-7

SOURCE 12 Plains Indian 'governments', 1841

The chief has no control over the life or limbs, or liberty of his subjects, nor no other power whatever, excepting that of *influence*. [This] he gains by his virtues and his exploits in war. In fact, he is no more than a *leader* whom every young warrior may follow, or . . . go back from . . . if he is willing to meet the disgrace that awaits him, who deserts his chief in the hour of danger.

Catlin, *Manners, Customs and Conditions of the North American Indians*, Vol. II, p. 239

SOURCE 13 'Tribal Government' described by Colonel Dodge, 1877

. . . [They have] their own very peculiar and eccentric ideas on the subject of government. . . .

I cannot say exactly how the powers and duties of these three governmental forms, [i.e. chiefs, councils and Dog Soldiers] blend and concur . . . and I have never met an Indian or white man who could satisfactorily explain them. The result, however, is fairly good, and seems well suited to the character, necessities and peculiarities of the life of the Plains Indians.

Dodge, *Hunting Grounds of the Great West*, p. 267

ABOVE: The Grand Chief of the Pawnees

A close-knit community

Their nomadic life not only meant that the Indians had to live in small bands, it also forced them to work together as a close-knit community. If the band was to be well fed, kept together during journeys, and defended in times of danger, men and women had to have their own tasks. They also had a responsibility to care for other members of the group. Because buffalo hunting involved both skill and danger it was the task of the younger and fitter men. Each hunt was strictly organised so that every hunter had a chance at the game and all members of the band, including the old and sick, had a fair share of the meat (source 14).

SOURCE 14 The bison hunt described by Black Elk, a Holy Man of the Oglala Sioux (born 1863)

We went on a big hunt after we had been at Willow Creek a while. One morning the crier came around the village calling out that we were going to break camp. The advisers were in the council tepee, and he cried to them: 'The advisers, come forth to the centre and bring your fires along'. It was their duty to save fire for the people, because we had no matches then. Then the crier said 'Many bison, I have heard! Your children, you must take care of them!' He meant to keep the children close while travelling, so that they would not scare the bison.

After we had been travelling a while, we came to a place where there were many turnips growing, and the crier said: 'Take off your loads and let your horses rest. Take your sticks and dig turnips for yourselves.' And while the people were doing this, the advisers sat on a hill nearby and smoked. Then the crier shouted: 'Put on your loads!' and soon the village was moving again.

When the sun was high, the advisers found a place to camp; and while the women were cooking, I heard people saying that the scouts were returning. Then the crier shouted: 'Your horses make ready! We shall go forth with arrows. Plenty of meat we shall make!'

RIGHT: The bison hunt by George Catlin

Then we started for where the bison were. The soldier band went first. They kept order and everybody had to obey. After them came the hunters. The people came up in the rear. Then the head man went around picking out the best hunters with the fastest horses, and to these he said: 'Young warriors, your work I know is good; so today you shall feed the helpless. Perhaps there are some old and feeble people without sons, or some who have little children and no man. You shall help these, and whatever you kill shall be theirs.' This was a great honour for young men. When the butchering was all over, they hung the meat across the horses' backs. On the way to the village all the hunting horses were loaded.

Then the advisers all went back into the council tepee, and from all directions the people came bringing gifts of meat to them. And when they had eaten all they could the crier shouted to the people: 'All come! It is more than I can eat!' And people came to get a little of the meat that was left over. The people feasted all night long and danced and sang. Those were happy times.

John G. Neihardt (ed.), *Black Elk Speaks*, Abacus/Sphere Books, 1974, pp. 47-50

BELOW: A young brave outside his tepee

Laws and punishments

In such a close community rigid rules about behaviour were unnecessary. There were no complicated ceremonies for marriage or divorce (source 15). A woman could divorce her husband by moving back to her parent's lodge. A Cheyenne husband could divorce his wife by throwing away a stick and shouting 'There goes my wife : I throw her away : whoever gets the stick may have her!'

Since all members of the band depended on each other so much, it was important that there should be as little quarrelling or ill-feeling as possible. The Indians, therefore, had to have the kind of punishments which would not split up the band.

So there were few strict laws and the bad opinion of the tribe was thought to be punishment enough for many crimes. Because they were nomads, the Indians obviously could not keep long term prisoners and so murder was punished in different ways. Some tribes banished murderers, others demanded compensation for the family of the victim (source 16).

The Indians often had to put the safety or survival of the whole band before that of individual members. This led them to adopt two customs which many white men could neither understand nor accept. To the Indians, however, polygamy and exposure of the aged were a matter of practical necessity (source 17).

SOURCE 15 The marriage of Geronimo, an Apache Indian

In 1846, being seventeen years of age, I was admitted to the council of warriors. When opportunity offered after this, I could go on the warpath with my tribe. This would be glorious. Perhaps the greatest joy to me was that now I could marry the fair Alope, daughter of No-po-so. She was a slender, delicate girl, but we had been lovers for a long time. So, I went to see her father. Perhaps our love was of no interest to him; perhaps he wanted to keep Alope with him; at any rate he asked many ponies for her. I made no reply but in a few days appeared before his wigwam with the herd of ponies and took with me Alope. This was all the marriage ceremony necessary in our tribe. Not far from my mother's tepee I had made for us a new home. Alope was a good wife. We followed the traditions of our fathers and were happy.

S. M. Barrett (ed.), *Geronimo: his own story*, Abacus/Sphere Books, 1974, p. 67

BELOW: A young Cheyenne girl

SOURCE 16 The customs of the Apaches described by Geronimo

If an Apache had allowed his aged parents to suffer for food or shelter, if he had neglected or abused the sick, if he had profaned our religion, or had been unfaithful, he might be banished from the tribe. The Apaches had no prisons as white men have. Instead of sending their criminals into prison they sent them out of their tribe. These faithless, cruel, lazy or cowardly members of the tribe were excluded in such a manner that they could not join any other tribe.

Barrett, *Geronimo*, p. 63

SOURCE 17 Polygamy and exposure, two Indian customs

Polygamy

The son of this chief, a youth of eighteen years distinguished himself by taking four wives in one day! Wishing to connect himself with some of the most influential men in the tribe, he had held an interview with one of the most distinguished, and made an arrangement for the hand of his daughter, for which he was given two horses, a gun, and several pounds of tobacco. He soon made similar arrangements with three other leading men of the tribe.

I visited the wigwam of this young man several times, and saw his four little wives seated round the fire, where all were entering very happily on the duties of married life. The ages of these young brides were probably all between twelve and fifteen years.

In this country polygamy is allowed, for where there are two or three times the number of women that there are of men, such an arrangement answers a good purpose; for so many of the females are taken care of.

Exposure

When we were about to start on our way from the village, my attention was directed to a very aged and emaciated man, who . . . was to be left to starve.

His friends and his children were preparing in a little time to be on the march. He had told them to leave him, 'He was old,' he said, 'and too feeble to march'. 'My children,' said he, 'our nation is poor, and it is necessary that you should all go to the country where you can get meat. My strength is no more, my days are nearly numbered, and I am a burden to my children. I cannot go, and I wish to die.'

This cruel custom of exposing their aged people, belongs to all the tribes who roam about the prairies, making severe marches, when such decrepit persons are totally unable to ride or walk. It often becomes absolutely necessary in such cases that they should be left; and they uniformly insist upon it, as this old man did.

Catlin, *Manners, Customs and Condition of the North American Indians*, Vol. I, pp. 213-217

Crafts and sports

The horse ensured such a plentiful supply of buffalo meat during the summer months that the Indians had time for leisure activities such as crafts and sports. Those tribes who lived for part of their year in semi-permanent villages developed skills in basket weaving and pottery. For the more nomadic tribes, who could only carry with them the necessities of daily living, these crafts were impossible. They became skilled at decorating their buffalo skin robes, tepees and their parflèches. The women especially liked to work geometric patterns with beads and quills. Often the patterns and colours had a symbolic meaning: red might mean thunder, a cross might mean a star.

Though the men often decorated their own robes, they preferred games and sports involving skill and chance. Their foot and horse races and shooting matches were, however, more than just amusements. They were essential activities which helped the young men to develop and improve their skills as horsemen, hunters and warriors (sources 18, 19).

BELOW: Indian art: a decorated Sioux cradle by George Catlin

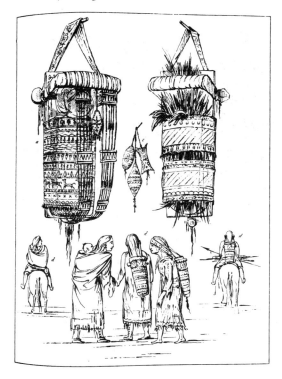

SOURCE 18 Astonishing feats of horsemanship amongst the Comanches

The Camanchees have many games, and in pleasant weather seem to be continually practising them. Racing horses is their principal mode of gambling. Amongst their feats of riding, there is one that has astonished me more than anything—a stratagem of war, learned and practised by every young man in the tribe; by which he is able to drop his body upon the side of the horse at the instant he is passing his enemies! In this condition he will hang whilst his horse is at fullest speed, rising and throwing his arrows over the horse's back, or under the horse's neck.

Catlin, Manners, Customs and Condition of the North American Indians, Vol. II, pp. 65-66

SOURCE 19 A game of arrow in a Mandan village

The young men assemble on the prairie, step forward in turn and shoot their arrows to see who can get the greatest number flying in the air at one time from the same bow. The most expert of them can get as many as eight arrows up before the first one reaches the ground.

For the successful use of the bow on horseback, at full speed, the great object of practice is to enable the bowman to draw the bow with suddenness and instant effect; and also to repeat the shots in the most rapid manner. When he leans quite low on his horse's side, and drives the arrow with astonishing force, the Indian is capable of producing instant death to the buffalo. I scarcely think it possible that any people can be found more skilled and capable of producing more deadly effects with the bow.

Catlin, Manners, Customs and Condition of the North American Indians, Vol. I, p. 140

TOP: A Comanche trick of war by Frederic Remington
ABOVE: An Indian horse race by George Catlin

Warfare and weapons

With the exception of the buffalo hunt, no activity was more important to the Indians than warfare. Preparations before a fight were as complicated as the celebrations which came after (source 20). As with all other aspects of an Indian's life, the whole aim of warfare and even its methods and tactics were influenced by three factors: the horse, the buffalo and the Great Plains environment. Moreover, it was because of this that the Indians' idea of warfare and tactics differed from that of many white men.

SOURCE 20 Preparing for war

All wars are decided on by the chiefs and doctors in council. After their resolve, the chief leads, his pipe with the reddened stem is sent through the tribe by his runners, and every man who consents to go to war, draws the smoke once through its stem. Then, the war dance is performed. Each warrior with weapons in hand, dances up and striking the reddened post, thereby takes the solemn oath not to desert his party. The chief leads in full dress to make himself as conspicuous a mark as possible for his enemy; whilst his men are chiefly denuded, and their limbs and faces covered with red earth, charcoal and grease, so as completely to disguise them.

At the close of hostilities, the two parties are often brought together by a flag of truce, where the chiefs sit in Treaty, smoking through the pipe of peace. After that, their warriors step forward, with the pipe of peace in the left hand, and the war-club in the right, and dance around in a circle, the 'pipe of peace dance'.

Catlin, *Manners, Customs and Condition of the North American Indians*, Vol. II, p. 242

The horse and the hunting ground

Before the coming of the whiteman all Indians had their traditional enemies amongst the other tribes. Throughout the 1830s, the Cheyennes and the Arapahos had fought the Comanches and Kiowas. In the north of the plains, Sioux had been at war with the Crows. The names and the places may have differed but the aim of their wars was always the same: to preserve their hunting grounds and above all else to capture horses. An Indian's fortune was counted in horses. His future (and his wife) would depend on them. For this reason, the stealthy capture of an enemy's most prized horses from the very door of his tepee became one of the finest feats of war (source 21). To a cowboy the stealing of another man's horse was a terrible crime (source 22).

BELOW: Colonel Dodge meets a Comanche war party

SOURCE 21 Comanche horse thieves described by Colonel Dodge, 1877

Where all are such magnificent thieves, it is difficult to decide which of the plains tribes deserves the palm for stealing. The Indians themselves give it to the Comanches, whose designation in the sign language of the plains is a forward, wriggling motion of the forefinger, signifying a snake, and indicating the silent stealth of that tribe. I have known a Comanche to crawl into a bivouac where a dozen men were sleeping, each with his horse tied to his wrist by the lariat, cut a rope within six feet of a sleeper's person, and get off with the horse without waking a soul.

Dodge, *Hunting Grounds of the Great West*, pp. 401ff

SOURCE 22 **The cowboy's view of horse stealing**

Some folks wonder at the cowman's code of honesty. As a rule he was honest as a woman's looking glass. There was hoss and cattle stealin' to be shore, and the Code of the West made a strange distinction between the two. To set a man afoot by stealin' his hoss carried a penalty of death, for deprivin' a man of his hoss could mean life itself on the plains. Public opinion regarded the cow as jes' property, and its theft was a case for the courts.

Ramon Adams, *The Old Time Cowhand*, Macmillan, 1961, pp. 56-7

BELOW: An Indian scalping his dead enemy: a white man's view, 1892

Braves and bravery

The Indians' idea of bravery also differed from that of some white men (source 23). Indians had no wish to die for a noble cause. Their first thought in war was to preserve their own lives: for an Indian brave was not merely a warrior, he was also a hunter and provider for his family. His needless death would bring hardship not glory to his band. Before the wars with the white men, the Plains Indians rarely made war with the main aim of killing their enemy or torturing prisoners. The taking of scalps was also not regarded by most tribes as an act of bravery, for scalping usually took place after death. The Crows and Sioux alone regarded a scalp as a first-class trophy (sources 24, 25).

For the Indian, personal glory was the greatest prize in war. This was won by brave deeds such as the rescue of an injured warrior or, most of all, the scoring of 'coups' by touching or striking a live enemy with a long stick (which became known as a coup stick).

SOURCE 23 **The Indian warrior as seen by Colonel Dodge, 1877**

His fighting is either the excitement of the charge or the desperation of despair; and, giving him every credit for physical prowess and personal bravery, there is yet in every Indian a total lack of that courage which prompts men to fight from a sense of duty...

For this there are two reasons; first, the Indian's lack of . . . that shoulder to shoulder courage which comes of discipline; and secondly, he is taught to risk life as seldom as possible, and that in all his exploits, craft is better than courage.

Dodge, *Hunting Grounds of the Great West*, p. 261-2

SOURCE 24 The reason for scalping, explained by Colonel Dodge, 1877

The Indian's idea of the future life in the Happy Hunting Ground is vague. All persons who die unscalped or unstrangled will meet in that final heaven. He goes there with the same wishes and needs. He will meet enemies whom, however, he strives to make as few as possible in that world by scalping as many as possible in this.

Dodge, *Hunting Grounds of the Great West*, p. 283

SOURCE 25 A modern historian compares the Indian's and the white man's treatment of captives

In western tradition, the Plains Indians are great torturers of captives (save the last bullet for yourself, pardner). However, researches have shown that captive torture was not traditional among the people of the plains, as it was among so many people of the eastern forest. Of course sadistic morons, both Indian and white, indulged in torture when they got the chance, as the wars worked up a really savage lather. But authentic records of official torture, so to speak, among the Plains Indians seem to be extremely rare. On the other hand, Indians regarded hanging, a custom generously practised by the military, as the most barbarous sort of death.

William Brandon, *The American Heritage Book of Indians*, Dell Publishing Co. Inc, 1974, p. 320

ABOVE: Celebrating victory: a scalp dance: an engraving from Colonel Richard Irving Dodge's book, 1877

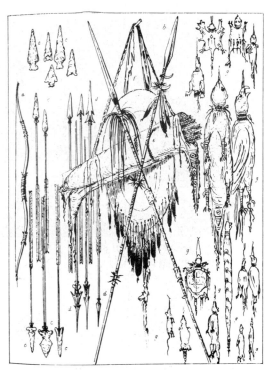

ABOVE: Indian weapons (left) and medicine bags (right) by George Catlin

Weapons and tactics

The weapons and tactics of the Indians were also determined by the horse and the Great Plains environment. Before the invention of the six-shooter and other rapid firing guns, the Indians' bows were an ideal weapon for fighting on horseback. Because of their skill and speed as horsemen and archers, the Indians preferred offensive warfare with swift attacks and rapid retreats. Defensive warfare was of so little interest to them that their camps were rarely defended. Since horse raiding parties often had to travel for as long as three weeks before reaching their enemies' camp, Indians usually went to war in summer and rarely in winter.

The Indians gained a detailed knowledge of the geography of the plains during their wanderings in search of the buffalo. This made them masters of guerrilla warfare which involved the use of small bands of warriors, ambushes and sudden attacks. To many white men this seemed like cowardice, stealth and treachery (sources 23, 26). To the Indians it was a matter of making the best possible use of their knowledge, skills and weapons.

SOURCE 26 Indian fighting described by Colonel Dodge, 1877

Their fights with each other are almost invariably surprises. . . . The first impulse of the Indian, on being surprised in his camp is that most natural to all animals—to scuttle away as fast as his legs will carry him.

In fighting with white men a surprise is always made possible. . . . When their very great superiority of numbers emboldens them to determine on [a pitched battle] . . . the different bands, each under its chief, are drawn up into an army, not a line. The Indians never receive a charge and very rarely meet one . . . the army . . . melts away into individual Indians. . . .

There is *one* well authenticated instance of a fair stand up fight between nearly equal numbers of [US] troops and Indians.

Dodge, *Hunting Grounds of the Great West*, pp. 371-2, 377-8

The spirit world of the Plains Indians

Spirits and 'medicine'

We have already seen the influence of their surroundings on the everyday life and customs of the Plains Indians. Yet the animals and landscape of the Great Plains also played an important part in shaping the ideas and beliefs of the Indians.

The Plains Indians lived close to nature and they believed that the events of the universe were governed by a series of controlling powers. The sun was the most important but the earth, the moon, the sky, rocks, wind and water also were thought to influence people and nature. The sun, the mountains, animals and even thunder all had their own mysterious life-force or 'medicine' (source 27). We must remember that the Indians lived an uncertain life. The comings and goings of the buffalo were irregular. The weather was also unpredictable. They could not tell when they might be short of food or when there would be a storm. So, what other explanation could there be for such mysterious happenings except the workings of spirits?

ABOVE: A Blackfoot Medicine Man by George Catlin. All tribes had Medicine Men who could contact the spirit world. Notice all the animal skins hanging from his costume

SOURCE 27 An Indian's explanation of thunder given to Francis Parkman, an explorer who visited a village of Oglala Sioux in 1846

'What is it,' said I, 'that makes the thunder?'

'It's my belief', said Reynal, 'that it's a big stone rolling over the sky'.

'Very likely,' I replied, 'but I want to know what the other Indians think about it'.

So he interpreted my question. There was a difference of opinion. At last old Red-Water looked up and said he had always known what the thunder was. It was a great black bird, and once he had seen it, in a dream, swooping down from the Black Hills, with its loud roaring wings; and when it flapped them over a lake, they struck lightning from the water.

Parkman, *The Oregon Trail*, pp. 231-3

ABOVE: A Buffalo Dance by
Remington

Ceremonies and dances

The Indians believed that the spirits in the wind, the thunder, the grass and the buffalo had power to do much good or great evil. They also believed that if they were to survive in this strange world they must take care to please the spirits and to ask for their help. In their daily lives therefore, the Indians were constantly performing small ceremonies in honour of these spirits (source 28). At other times the whole band held great ceremonies. These were often ritual dances which Indians hoped would ensure the return of the buffalo each spring (source 29). Music (especially the low tones of the drums or the shrill notes of a flute) was thought to have the power to call or to please the spirits and so each dance was always accompanied by its own music.

Spirit friends

When a boy was approaching manhood, the time came for him to get in touch with the spirit world by means of a dream. During this dream he would be given a guardian spirit, usually a bird or animal, and also a secret song by means of which he could contact his spirit friend (source 30).

To the Indians their religion was an integral part of life. It helped to ensure a continuing supply of food. It protected them against accidents and evil happenings and it provided them with many practical benefits. To many white men however, it was a sign of ignorance and superstition (source 31).

SOURCE 28 'The duty of prayer' by Ohiyesa, a Santee Sioux physician

In the life of the Indian there was only one duty—the duty of prayer. Whenever the red hunter comes upon a scene that is strikingly beautiful: the rainbow's glowing arch above the mountain, a vast prairie tinged with the blood-red of sunset—he pauses for an instant in worship. He sees no need for setting apart one day in seven as a holy day, since to him all days are God's.

Eastman (Ohiyesa), *The Soul of the Indian*, in T. C. McLuhan, *Touch the Earth*, Abacus/Sphere, 1973, p. 361

SOURCE 29 The Mandan Buffalo Dance, described by George Catlin

For the most part of the year, the young hunters can kill meat in abundance. There are other seasons also when the young men have ranged about the country without finding meat . . .

The chief issues his order to his runners who proclaim it through the village—and in a few minutes the dance begins. About ten or fifteen Mandans at a time join in the dance, each one with the skin of the buffalo's head [or mask] with the horns on, placed over his head, and in his hand his favourite bow or lance, with which he is used to slay the buffalo.

This dance never fails, nor can it, for it cannot be stopped (but is going incessantly day and night) until 'buffalo come'. Drums are beating and rattles are shaken, and songs and yells are shouted, and on-lookers stand ready with masks on their heads, and weapons in hand, to take the place of each one as he becomes fatigued.

During this time 'lookers' are kept on the hills in the neighbourhood of the village. When they discover buffaloes in sight they give the signal, by 'throwing their robes'. At this joyful intelligence, there is a shout of thanks to the Great Spirit! These dances have sometimes been continued in this village two and three weeks without stopping.

Catlin, *Manners, Customs and Condition of the North American Indians*, Vol. I, pp. 127-8

SOURCE 30 A Blackfoot chief describes a young Indian's vision to the Rev. F. Wilson in the 1880s

Young men go up on to a hill, and cry and pray for some animal or bird to come to them. For five or six days they neither eat nor drink, and they become thin. While in this state they dream, and whatever animal or bird they see in their dreams becomes their medicine or guardian through life. They are also told in a dream what description of herbs or roots to gather as their medicine, and this they collect and put carefully into a small bag to keep as a charm. They also kill the animal that they dreamed of, and keep its skin as a charm. No one knows what is the medicine they have gathered; it is kept a secret. The little bag is kept in the tent, and no one may touch it but the owner.

Sir J. G. Frazer, *The Native Races of America*, Lund Humphries, 1939, p. 138

SOURCE 31 A highly religious being: Catlin's view of the Indian

I have heard it said by some very good men, and some who have been preaching the Christian religion amongst them, that Indians have no religion but only ignorant superstition. I assert that the North American Indian is everywhere, in his native state, a highly moral and religious being. I never saw any other people who spend so much of their lives in humbling themselves before, and worshipping the Great Spirit.

Catlin, *Manners, Customs and Condition of the North American Indians*, Vol. II, pp. 242-4

ABOVE: A highly religious being

'Children of the earth': the values of the Plains Indians

We have now looked at the many ways in which the environment of the Great Plains affected the customs and beliefs of the Plains Indians. Finally, let us consider how their surroundings also influenced their values—in other words, their ideas about the most important things in life.

To some people this might mean making money, collecting possessions or helping others. The Indians no doubt thought that hunting and fighting, care of the family, and the survival of the band and the tribe to be important. Beyond this, however, there was yet another thing of great importance in their lives and this was their feeling of being close to nature.

A kinship with nature

The Indians may often have felt afraid in the face of natural phenomena—afraid of thunder, afraid that the buffalo might not return. But unlike many white men they lived most of their lives in the open, near to birds, trees, animals and plants. They had time to observe these closely and came to feel a kinship with all creatures. Unlike most white men, Indians did not believe that men were the most important beings on the earth—plants and animals were just as important (source 32). This feeling of being close to nature showed itself in small matters of everyday life (sources 33-4).

SOURCE 32 Kinship with nature: Black Elk, Holy Man of the Oglala Sioux, describes his beliefs

My friend, I am going to tell you the story of my life. It is the story of all life that is holy and is good to tell, and of us two leggeds sharing it with the four leggeds and the wings of the air—all green things; for these are children of one mother (the earth) and their father is one spirit.

You have noticed that everything an Indian does is in a circle and that is because the Power of the World always works in circles. The sky is round and I have heard that the earth is round like a ball. The wind, in its greatest power, whirls. Birds make their nests in circles. Even the seasons form a great circle and always come back again to where they were. The life of a man is a circle from childhood to childhood. Our tepees were round like the nests of the birds and these were always set in a circle.

Neihardt, *Black Elk Speaks*, pp. 13, 19

BELOW: A sacred circle: sun dance lodge

SOURCE 33 Indian seasons, described by Black Elk

January	Moon of Frost in the Tepee
February	Moon of the Dark Red Calves
March	Moon of the Snow Blind
April	Moon of the Red Grass appearing
May	Moon when the Ponies shed
June	Moon of Making Fat
July	Moon of the Red Cherries
August	Moon when the Cherries turn Black
September	Moon when the Calves grow Hair
October	Moon of the Changing Season
November	Moon of the Falling Leaves
December	Moon of the Popping Trees

Neihardt, *Black Elk Speaks*

SOURCE 34 The Indian's feelings for nature and the earth: told by Chief Luther Standing Bear of the Sioux (born 1868)

The Sioux was a true lover of nature. He loved the earth and all things of the earth. . . . Their tepees were built upon the earth. The birds that flew in the air came to rest upon the earth and it was the final abiding place of all things that lived and grew. . . . Kinship with all creatures of the earth, sky and water was a real and active [belief]. . . .

The old Sioux was wise. He knew that man's heart away from nature becomes hard; he knew that lack of respect for growing, living things soon led to lack of respect for humans too.

Chief Luther Standing Bear, *Land of the Spotted Eagle*, Houghton Mifflin, 1933, pp. 192-7

ABOVE: A sacred circle: Medicine Wheel, Medicine Mountain (Wyoming)
BELOW: Arapaho pouch with sacred circle target design

'I love that land more than all the rest of the world'

The Indians also developed a special feeling for their land (their hunting grounds on the plains) and the earth. To the Indians, land was something that no man could own or buy or sell or fence off. The earth belonged to all people, animals and plants (sources 35-6). The Indians' attitude towards land was the one which white men found most difficult to understand. In the end it led to bitter fighting between them, as we shall see later (source 37).

RIGHT: Medicine Bluff Creek: a sacred place of the Indians

SOURCE 35 A Blackfoot chief compares the white man's and the Indian's attitude to the land

Our land is more valuable than your money. It will not even perish by the flames of fire. As long as the sun shines, and the waters flow, this land will be here to give life to men and animals. We cannot sell the lives of men and animals; therefore, we cannot sell this land. It was put here for us by the Great Spirit and we cannot sell it because it does not belong to us.

Dee Brown, *Bury my Heart at Wounded Knee*, Holt, Rinehart and Winston, 1970, p. 316

**SOURCE 36 'The dust and blood of our ancestors':
Chief Joseph of the Nez Percés describes his feeling for his land**

My father sent for me. I saw he was dying. He said 'My son, my body is returning to my mother earth. Always remember that your father never sold his country. A few years more, and white men will be all around you. They have their eyes on this land. My son, never forget my dying words. This country holds your father's body. Never sell the bones of your father and your mother'.

My father smiled and passed away to the spirit land. I buried him in that beautiful valley of winding waters. I love that land more than all the rest of the world. A man who would not love his father's grave is worse than a wild animal.

Helen Addison Howard, *War Chief Joseph*, Caxton Printers, 1941, p. 85

SOURCE 37 'Lo! The Poor Indian', Horace Greeley's comment on the Plains Indians and their attitude to land, 1859

The average Indian of the prairies is a being who does little credit to human nature. As I passed over those magnificent bottoms of Kansas which form the reservations of the Delaware, Potawatomies, etc.—the very best cornlands on earth—and saw their owners sitting around the doors of their lodges at the height of the planting season and I could not help saying, 'These people must die out—there is no help for them. God has given this earth to those who will subdue and cultivate it.'

Greeley, *New York to San Francisco*, 1859, pp. 119-20

BELOW: 'Okolohama': last home of the Indians

2
The first American settlers in the West 1840 - 1865

The United States and the West in 1840

In 1840 less than half the land west of the Mississippi actually belonged to the United States. A large area of the Great Plains had been purchased from the French in 1803, but forty years later few American settlers lived there. The plains were still, as we have seen, the hunting grounds of the Indians.

In the south of the Great Plains there was the independent Republic of Texas. Until the mid 1830s Texas had been part of the Mexican Republic, but in the revolution of 1835-6 American settlers there had fought and won their freedom. However, ten years passed before Texas became a state of the Union. In the meantime Texans were citizens of the 'Lone Star Republic' with its own government, its own president and its own lawmen, the 'Texas Rangers'.

The land west of Texas between the southern Rockies and the Pacific still belonged to Mexico in 1840. This area included the coastlands of California, then the home of Indians, Mexican ranchers and American fur traders.

Finally in the North West lay 'the Oregon Country'. Officially this area was jointly occupied by Great Britain and the United States, but in 1840 the only inhabitants of the area were the native Indians, some British and American fur traders and a handful of American farmers and missionaries.

The close of 'The Frontier' in 1890

By 1890 the western boundary of the United States was the Pacific Ocean (see

OPPOSITE: The Californian gold rush

map, p. 39). In that year the Superintendent of the Census announced that the country's 'unsettled area has been so broken into isolated bodies of settlement that there can hardly be said to be a frontier line'. Although many regions were still sparsely populated, most of the American West had been organised into states of the Union. But how, when and why did this remarkable and rapid process of settlement take place?

The territorial expansion of the USA 1776-1853

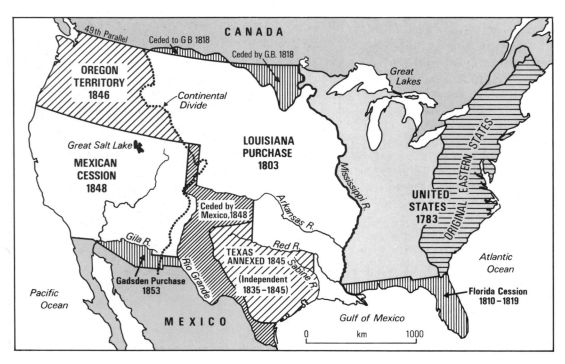

Settlement of 'The Fertile Fringes'

The first areas of the West to attract large numbers of American settlers were, in the whiteman's view, 'the fertile fringes': Texas, Oregon and California.

'Gone to Texas!'

When Texas became a republic in 1836, 30 000 immigrants from the eastern states had settled there. After the economic depression of 1837 the number of immigrants increased rapidly till by 1850 the state of Texas (which joined the Union in 1845) had over 200 000 inhabitants including 58 000 slaves. Most of these settlers were small farmers. They were attracted by the offer of free land in the river valleys of southern Texas which could be cultivated by the same techniques used on farms in the East. 'Gone to Texas!' came to be a familiar slogan scrawled on the barns of abandoned farms in Missouri, Kentucky and Tennessee.

The Oregon Trail

In 1840 there were less than 150 Americans in 'the Oregon Country'. Then, in 1843 the first wagon train managed to cross the Great Plains and the Rockies to reach the Columbia River. This marked a turning point in Oregon's history. Until a trail for wagons was opened up, mass emigration to the Pacific coastlands of the North West was impossible.

In the following years 'Oregon Fever' hit the eastern states. In 1844, 1500 new settlers made their way along the Oregon Trail, a journey of over 3200 kilometres (see map, p. 41). Some of these pioneers were 'trailblazers' attracted by the excitement of opening up a new country. Most, however, were farmers driven west by poor prices for farm products in the East. They were attracted by reports of the fertile farming lands in the Willamette Valley.

By 1845, 6000 Americans lived in Oregon Country compared with only 750 British settlers—and many more were to follow. In 1846 the British government agreed to give up its claims to land south of the 49th parallel (see map, p. 38). Two years later Oregon became a territory of the United States of America.

LEFT: On the Oregon trail

California and the Gold Rush

The first wagons crossed the Sierra Nevada mountains in 1844 and entered the Sacramento valley of California. But for the next four years fewer settlers went to California than to Oregon. The route was more hazardous and no reliable Emigrants' Guide had yet been produced. The outbreak of the war with Mexico in May 1846 also discouraged settlers. The Mexicans were not willing to give up either California or Texas to the Americans without a fight. The war lasted only eighteen months but in 1847 less than 100 wagons headed for California. The Mexicans were defeated and in January 1848 they ceded

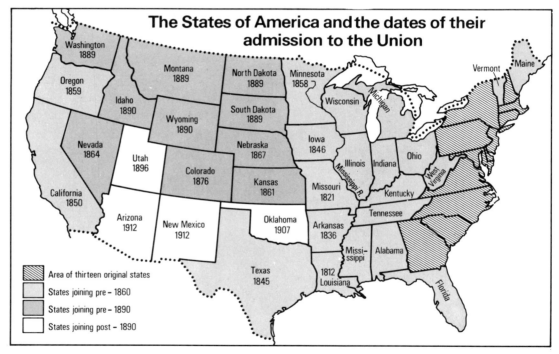

The States of America and the dates of their admission to the Union

Washington 1889
Oregon 1859
Idaho 1890
Montana 1889
North Dakota 1889
Minnesota 1858
Wisconsin
Michigan
Vermont
Maine
Wyoming 1890
South Dakota 1889
Nevada 1864
Utah 1896
Colorado 1876
Nebraska 1867
Iowa 1846
Illinois
Indiana
Ohio
West Virginia
California 1850
Arizona 1912
New Mexico 1912
Kansas 1861
Missouri 1821
Kentucky
Oklahoma 1907
Arkansas 1836
Tennessee
Missi-ssippi
Alabama
Texas 1845
1812 Louisiana
Florida

Mississippi R.

Area of thirteen original states
States joining pre – 1860
States joining pre – 1890
States joining post – 1890

the provinces of Upper California and New Mexico to the USA and recognised the new State of Texas. Then in September 1848 news broke in the East of the discovery of gold in California earlier that year. Within two months sixty ships were on their way to California via Cape Horn. In spring 1849 a reported 40 000 gold diggers were heading westwards overland on the California Trail. Others used the Santa Fé Trail (see map, p. 41). By August the new Californians had chosen a governor and a legislature. The following year they became a State of the Union with a population rapidly outstripping that of Oregon (see Fig. 1).

Fig. 1 The population of California and Oregon, 1848-60

Year	California	Oregon
1848	14 000	12 000
1850	100 000	
1852	250 000	
1860	380 000	52 000

LEFT: A mining camp in Nevada near Carson City in the 1880s

The miners and the mountains

In the early 1840s American emigrants settled in areas of the West where they could farm and live as they had done in the East. After 1849, gold in California proved an even greater attraction for many people. To reach California and Oregon, emigrants were prepared to face a wagon journey lasting several months, with all the difficulties and dangers this involved.

At this stage no one even thought of settling in the area between the Far West and East. The plains were still regarded as a desert, the mountains as both dangerous and inhospitable. Yet by 1860 American settlers had also moved into the mountain region. The people who came here had good reasons not to mind the steep mountains and the barren plateaux.

One such group of settlers were the miners. They actually came in search of the rock outcrops which shielded mineral bearing lodes. By the 1850s the easy surface diggings in California had been almost worked out. The gold which remained had to be crushed from quartz or extracted from beds 30 metres below the surface. Metal crushing mills and mine shafts cost money. Gold mining continued but with capital and machines provided by eastern businessmen. Thousands of individual prospectors were left without a living.

A new gold rush

Then in 1858-9 gold was discovered in the mountain and plateau regions of what would become Colorado and Nevada (see map, right). A new gold rush began. As before, prospectors set off from the eastern states and travelled west. 'Pike's Peak or Bust!' was the familiar phrase written on the canvas of miners' wagons. But thousands more prospectors left California and headed back east into the mountains.

In the following years gold and silver were found elsewhere in the mountain region; in Idaho (1860), Montana (1862), Arizona (1863) and the Black Hills of Dakota (1874) (see map, right). Wherever gold was discovered, not only mines but also mining camps grew up. In time many became thriving towns such as Virginia City and Denver. The miners needed food and manufactured goods and so cattlemen, traders and other people were soon attracted to the region. The demands of the mining areas for improved transportation also spurred on the building of a transcontinental railway.

The development of mining greatly accelerated the settlement of the West including the Great Plains, as we shall see later. The miners are also interesting in that many of them were the first frontiersmen to move not in the usual pattern from east to west but also from west to east.

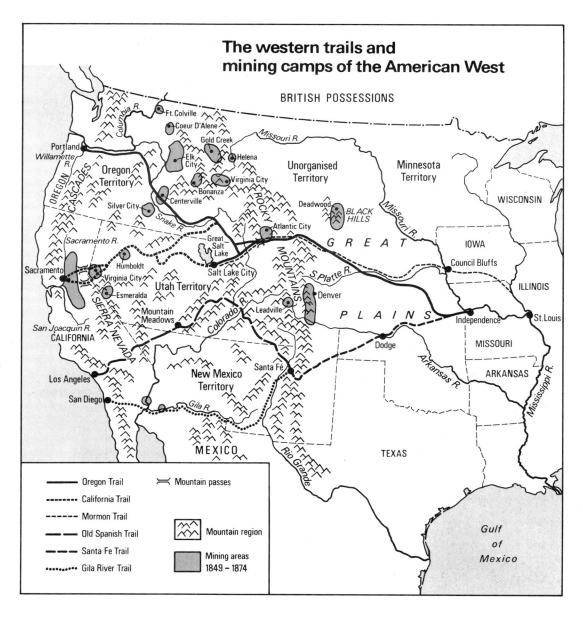

The western trails and mining camps of the American West

Legend:
— Oregon Trail
---- California Trail
-- Mormon Trail
— — Old Spanish Trail
— · — Santa Fe Trail
······ Gila River Trail
⤫ Mountain passes
Mountain region
Mining areas 1849 – 1874

The Mormons and Salt Lake City

Introduction

The second group of settlers to decide to move into the mountain region of the American West was the Mormons.

SALT LAKE CITY.

BRIGHAM YOUNG

PREACHING   PROPOSED MORMON TEMPLE   ONLY SIX WIVES

In July 1847 they began to build their first settlement in the valley of the Great Salt Lake in the Great Basin region of the mountains. It became known as Salt Lake City.

In this case study we shall consider the following questions about the Mormons and their great decision:

Who were the Mormons and where did they come from?

Why did the Mormons decide to leave their homes in the East and settle in the heart of the mountain region of the West?

What problems did they have to face as a result of their decision and how did they overcome them?

Who were the Mormons and where did they come from?

Joseph Smith

The Mormons were members of a religious sect called 'The Church of Jesus Christ of Latter Day Saints'. This Church was first established in June 1830 by Joseph Smith, the son of a poor Vermont farmer. In 1823, when Joseph Smith was only 17, he reported that he had had a visitation from an angel of God. The angel's name was Moroni. Moroni had told Joseph to dig in the soil on a hillside near his home

in Palmyra, New York. In the hole, Joseph said he had discovered a set of gold plates. But Moroni forbade Joseph to remove the plates for four years. Then on 22 September 1827 the angel at last 'delivered the records' into Joseph's hands. Here is Joseph Smith's own account of what he found:

SOURCE 38 Letter to 'Times and Seasons Magazine', Nauvoo, 1 March 1842

These records were engraven on plates which had the appearance of gold. Each plate was six inches [15 cm] wide and eight inches [20 cm] long and not quite so thick as common tin. They were filled with engravings, in Egyptian characters and bound together in a volume, as the leaves of a book, with three rings running through the whole. The volume was something near . . . [15 cm] . . . in thickness. The whole book exhibited many marks of antiquity in its construction and much skill in the art of engraving. With the records was found a curious instrument which the ancients called 'Urim and Thummim', which consisted of two transparent stones set in the rim of a bow [like a pair of crystal spectacles]. I translated the record by the gift and power of God.

W. Mulder and A. R. Mortensen (eds.), *Amongst the Mormons, Historic Accounts by Contemporary Observers*, Alfred A. Knopf, 1958, pp. 12-13

The story of the gold plates

The plates recounted the history of the tribes of Israel which were said to have migrated to America centuries before Christ. After their arrival the tribes split into warring groups. These fought for hundreds of years until Christ 'made his appearance upon this Continent [i.e. America] . . . [and] planted his gospel here in all its fulness . . . [and appointed] . . .

apostles, prophets, pastors and teachers'. Later, however, the fighting was resumed until the great battle of Cumorah circa AD 384. Amongst the few survivors of the battle were a man named Mormon and his son Moroni. Mormon and Moroni spent the rest of their lives recording the story of their people on the golden plates. Whoever found the plates was ordered to restore the true Church of Jesus Christ in America and build up God's Kingdom on earth before Christ reappeared to begin a thousand-year reign.

The Book of Mormon

Moroni had warned Joseph Smith that only he was allowed to view the plates. So Smith dictated their story to his wife and a few friends who sat out of sight of the plates behind a strung-up blanket. In March 1830 Joseph Smith published the work under the title of *The Book of Mormon,* because the plates had been chiefly engraved by Mormon, the father of Moroni.

The book is similar in its style and themes to the Old Testament. Together with the Bible ('as far as it is correctly

LEFT: Facsimile of a section of the gold plates said to have been copied out on paper by Joseph Smith
BELOW: The Mormon temple at Kirtland, Ohio

translated'—by Smith) and Smith's later revelations, the *Book of Mormon* was to form the central text for members of the new Mormon Church.

The Latter Day Saints

When the book was first published, Joseph Smith had only five converts to his new Church. Yet within a year he had over a thousand followers. The 'Saints' soon became more than just another religious sect. They became a close-knit community.

In return for their total obedience the 'Saints' were promised that they would be the chosen people of God, both on earth and in heaven. In 1831 the town of Kirtland in Ohio was chosen by the Mormons as their new 'Zion', or City of God. Converts flocked to join the 'Saints'. They set up farms and homes and began to build a great temple. Joseph Smith was even tempted by the speculative fever of the early 1830s—he set up a Mormon bank.

Why did the Mormons decide to 'Go West'?

Problems in Kirtland

In 1831 it seemed that everything was going well for Joseph Smith and his 'Latter Day Saints'. But gradually trouble and ill feeling began to arise between the Mormons and the settlers around Kirtland.

ABOVE: Joseph Smith—tarred and feathered

Matters came to a head in March 1832 when Joseph Smith was dragged from his bed one night and tarred and feathered by a mob from a nearby town. This was the first of many outbreaks of violence connected with the Mormons over the next fourteen years.

Despite this incident, Smith and many of his followers stayed on in Kirtland until the financial panic of 1837. In that year Smith's bank collapsed together with many other banks, leaving huge debts. Many of the Mormons who had invested their life savings in the bank turned against Smith. But their anger was slight compared with that of his Gentile [non-Mormon] creditors. According to the sworn statement of one witness, Smith claimed that he had founded the bank because God had told him 'to milk the Gentiles'. The Mormon world at Kirtland collapsed. Smith and his remaining supporters fled westwards to join other Mormon settlements recently set up in Missouri.

Conflict in Missouri

Smith arrived in Missouri a bitter man, convinced that Gentile persecution was the real reason for all his troubles. He decided that the Mormons would survive only if they met force with force—talk which soon aroused the hostility of other settlers in Missouri. Trouble broke out again between the Mormons and their neighbouring settlers. Here is Joseph Smith's account of what happened:

BELOW: Mormon troubles in Missouri

SOURCE 39 **Violence against the Mormons**

A considerable settlement was formed in Jackson County. Numbers joined the church and we were increasing rapidly. We made large purchases of land, our farms teemed with plenty, and peace and happiness was enjoyed throughout our neighbourhood. But as we could not associate with our neighbours (who were many of them the basest of men and had fled from the face of civilised society to the frontier country to escape the hand of justice) in their midnight revels, their sabbath breaking, horse racing and gambling, they commenced at first to ridicule, then to persecute us. Finally an organised mob assembled and burned our houses, tarred and feathered, and whipped many of our brethren and finally drove them from their habitations.

This proceeding was winked at by the government, and although we had deeds for our land and had violated no law, we could obtain no redress.

Many of our brethren removed to Clay [county] where they continued until 1836, three years. There was no violence but there were threatenings of violence. But in the summer of 1836, these threatenings began to assume a more serious form. After much violence, privation and loss of property we were again driven from our homes.

BELOW: An attack on the Mormons at Haun's mill
LEFT: Lieutenant-General Joseph Smith: prophet, seer and revelator

We next settled in Caldwell and Davies counties, where we made large and extensive settlements, thinking to free ourselves from oppression, by settling in new counties, with very few inhabitants in them. But here we were not allowed to live in peace. In 1838 we were again attacked by mobs, an exterminating order was issued by Gov. Boggs, and organised banditti ranged through the country, robbed us of our cattle, sheep, horses, hogs etc. Many of our people were murdered in cold blood, the chastity of our women was violated, and we were forced to sign away our property at the point of the sword. From twelve to fifteen thousand souls—men, women and children—were driven from their own fire sides, and from the lands in the depth of winter to wander as exiles on the earth.
Mulder and Mortensen, *Amongst the Mormons*, pp. 14-15

The Mormons as seen through the eyes of Missouri settlers

To Smith and his followers, this persecution seemed unjustified. But the Missouri settlers felt they had good reason to distrust the Mormons and to force them to move to another area. They felt threatened by the Mormons, their religion and different way of life. These extracts from a local newspaper tell us some of the reasons why people feared and resented the Mormons:

SOURCE 40

But little more than two years ago, some two or three of these people made their appearance on the Upper Missouri and they now number some 1200 souls in this country. Each autumn and spring pours forth its swarm among us, flooding us with the very dregs. Elevated as they mostly are but little above the condition of our blacks, they have become a subject of much anxiety. Well grounded complaints have been already made of their corrupting influence on our slaves.

We are told that we [the Gentiles] of this country are to be cut off, and our lands taken over by them for inheritances. Whether this is to be accomplished by the hand of our destroying Angel, the judgements of God, or by force, they are not fully agreed among themselves. . . . It requires no gift of prophecy to tell that the day is not far distant, when the government of the county will be in their hands, when the sheriff, the Justices, and the county judges will be Mormons. What would be the fate of our lives and property, in the hands of jurors and witnesses who do not blush to swear that they have wrought miracles and supernatural cures; have converse with God and his Angels and are fired with the prospect of gaining inheritances without price?

One of the means resorted to by them, in order to drive us to emigrate, is an invitation to the free brethren of colour [i.e. freed slaves] in Illinois to come . . . to claim the rights of citizenship.

Of their pretended revelations from Heaven —the maladies they pretend to heal by laying on of hands—and the contemptible gibberish with which they profane the Sabbath we have nothing to say. Vengeance belongs to God alone.

Missouri Intelligencer and Boon's Lick Advertiser, 10 August 1833

Rumours began to circulate of a Mormon secret society, the *Danites*, who were planning to persuade the Indians to join the Mormons in a war against the people of Missouri. Another group, the destruction company, was to be specially trained in burning and wrecking.

The Mormons at Nauvoo

'The Mormons must be treated as enemies', announced the Governor of Missouri, 'and must be exterminated or driven from the state, if necessary, for the public peace'. In 1838, for the second time in six years the Mormons were forced to leave their homes and find a new settlement.

At this time Smith was unwilling to move further west since this would mean entering the 'Great American Desert', and so the Mormons headed north east to Illinois. Here they deliberately chose a site in a swampy lowland which had been avoided by earlier settlers. Joseph Smith described what happened to the Mormons in Illinois:

SOURCE 41

We arrived in the state of Illinois in 1839 where we found a friendly home. We have commenced to build a city called 'Nauvoo' in Hancock County. We number from six to eight thousand here, besides vast numbers in the country around and in almost every county of the state. We have a city charter granted us and a charter for a legion of troops of which now number 1500. We have also a charter for a university, for an agricultural and manufacturing society, we have our own laws and administrators, and possess all the privileges that other free and enlightened citizens enjoy.

Persecution has not stopped the progress of truth, but has only added fuel to the flames; it has spread with increasing rapidity.

Times and Seasons Magazine, Nauvoo, 1 March 1842

Polygamy and politics

As we can see from Joseph Smith's account, the same thing happened in Nauvoo as in Missouri. The Illinois settlers at first welcomed the Mormons and then began to feel threatened by them. They were afraid of a people who set themselves up as an independent state with their own laws, their own privileges, and their own private army. Stories began to circulate amongst both Saints and Gentiles about Smith's greed, his speculation in land and the counterfeiting of money. Gentiles in Nauvoo complained that the Mormons 'stole, robbed and plundered from all their neighbours, and all the time'. Then two further developments took place which alarmed the Illinois settlers even more. This letter, written by a young Gentile girl living in Nauvoo in 1843, tells us what they were:

SOURCE 42

Nauvoo, Sept. 8 1843
My dear friends at home,

We hear that Joseph has already had some wonderful revelations not yet made public, but that a few of the elders put their heads together and whisper. What it is we can only surmise by faint rumours. A month ago, one of the Apostles . . . returned from a two years' mission in England, bringing with him a wife and child, although he had left a wife and family here when he went away. I am

ABOVE LEFT: A first view of polygamy: a Mormon settler with his wives and children
ABOVE: The murder of Joseph Smith

told that his first wife is reconciled to this. Her husband and some others have reasoned with her that plurality of wives is taught in the Bible, that Abraham and all the old prophets, had several wives, and if right for them, it is right for the Latter Day Saints.

I cannot believe that Joseph will ever sanction such a doctrine. Should the Mormons in any way engraft such an article on their religion, the sect would surely fall to pieces.

Last winter when Joseph was in the meshes of the law, he was assisted by some politicians of the Whig party, to whom he pledged himself in the coming elections. Now he wants the Democratic party to win, and as it is revealed for him to vote, so go over all the Mormons like sheep following the bell sheep over a wall. Nauvoo, with its 15 000 inhabitants, has a vote that tells in the State elections, and all summer politicians, able men of both parties, have been here making speeches, caressing and flattering.

Your affectionate sister,
Charlotte

'A Girl's Letters from Nauvoo', first published in *Overland Monthly*, San Francisco, December 1890

The murder of Joseph Smith

The political power of the Mormons was obviously a matter of great concern to many Illinois settlers. The news that Joseph Smith intended to stand for President of the United States was even more disturbing. But the rumour that the Mormons had begun to practise polygamy was the last straw. Illinois settlers felt that it was immoral, corrupting, irreligious and a threat to the very basis of their society; the idea of home, family and one man to one woman. Many must also have feared that polygamy would lead to a rapid increase in the Mormon population. The Whig party who had previously supported Smith turned against the Mormons and they were left surrounded by angry and frightened enemies.

To survive in Nauvoo the Mormons had to remain united. But Joseph Smith's revelation about polygamy caused a split amongst the Saints. One group set up their own newspaper to attack Joseph Smith's political ambitions and his ideas on polygamy. When Joseph Smith ordered the printing press to be destroyed, he and his brother Hyrum were arrested and put in jail in the town of Carthage. Mass meetings were held calling for a 'war of extermination' on the Mormons. Then on 27 June 1844, a mob stormed the jail and killed Joseph Smith and his brother. To the people of Illinois this was only the beginning. The Illinois legislature revoked the special charter granting independence to the citizens of Nauvoo. More threats of violence were made against other Mormons. Finally, the Governor of Illinois proposed that the Mormons should leave the state.

Brigham Young and the decision to move West

It now became clear to the Mormons that they would never be safe so long as they lived within the United States. But where could they go? The man who made this decision was Brigham Young, who became the new President of the Church after Smith's murder.

Brigham Young was born in 1801 and, like Smith, grew up in Vermont. In later years he became a carpenter and glazier. Young joined the Mormon Church in 1832 and soon became a leading official. In

RIGHT: Brigham Young

1838 when the Mormons were forced to leave Missouri, Young, as the senior member of the Quorum of the Twelve Apostles, organised the move to Nauvoo. In the following year he went to England and established a Mormon Mission and newspaper, baptising 9000 converts and distributing 5000 copies of the *Book of Mormon.*

In 1844 Young was in Boston leading Smith's campaign for the Presidency. On learning the news of the prophet's death, he returned to Nauvoo and soon gained control of the Church. Brigham Young had the qualities and experience the Mormons now most needed. He was, as a later biographer, H. E. Bolton wrote, 'a devout believer, but more especially a lion-hearted man of iron will, an *organiser* and the founder of a commonwealth'. From this time until his death in August 1877, Brigham Young dominated the Mormon Church and his schemes were to have great influence on its history and development. Young decided that the Mormons had no alternative but to leave Nauvoo and head west towards the only un-inhabited area left, the Great Plains and the Rocky Mountains. A circular of the Mormon High Council published on 20 January 1846 informed the 'Saints' of the decision of Brigham Young and the Church leaders:

SOURCE 43 Decisions made

Beloved Brethren and Friends, We, the members of the High Council of the Church, have unanimously agreed . . . to inform you that we intend to set out into the west country from this place some time in the early part of the month of March. . . . We agreed to leave the country for the sake of peace, upon the condition that no more vexatious prosecutions be instituted against us. But there are some who are unwilling that we should have an existence anywhere. But your destinies are in the hands of God and so also is theirs.

Charles Mackay, *The Mormons or Latter Day Saints with Memoirs of the Life and Death of Joseph Smith, the American Mahomet*, London, 1851

Problems, difficulties and solutions

The decision to leave Nauvoo was not a simple and straightforward one. It would, indeed, solve one problem—the 'persecution' of the Mormons in Illinois. But in turn it created several more problems, all of which had to be solved. First, where exactly could they go? Secondly, how would they get there? Thirdly, what kind of life would they be able to make for themselves when they arrived in this unknown place?

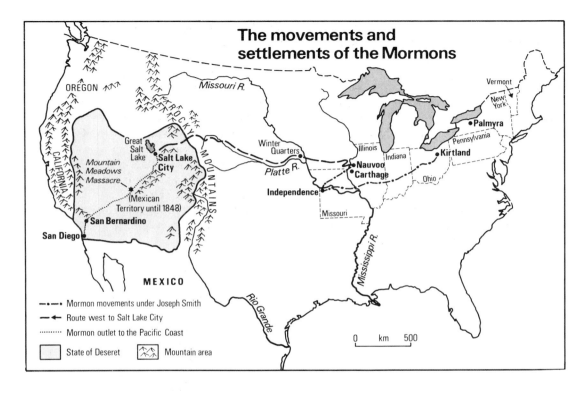

The movements and settlements of the Mormons

-·-·- Mormon movements under Joseph Smith

-◄-◄- Route west to Salt Lake City

········ Mormon outlet to the Pacific Coast

State of Deseret   Mountain area

0   km   500

Where to go?

Brigham Young believed that if they were to escape further persecution, then the Saints had to settle in a place outside the United States and where no one else would ever wish to live. He had already read with interest the descriptions written by explorers of the Rocky Mountain region. It was clear to him that no Mormon settlement in the northern Rockies would be safe since travellers had already begun to make their way up the Oregon Trail. The southern region of the Rockies, however, was different. In 1846 this still belonged to Mexico and so was beyond the jurisdiction of the US government. Furthermore the mountains here were especially forbidding to settlers. On 9 August 1846, Brigham Young told President Polk of the Mormons' decision.

SOURCE 44

[The Mormons are embarking on] a journey which we design shall end in a location west of the Rocky Mountains and within the basin of the Great Salt Lake, or Bear river valley, as soon as circumstances shall permit, believing that to be a point where a good living will require hard labour, and consequently will be coveted by no other people, while it is surrounded by so unpopulous but fertile a country.

Mulder and Mortensen, *Amongst the Mormons*, p. 209

How to get there?

Preparations for the journey

The basin of the Great Salt Lake seemed safe enough, but it was over 2250 kilometres west of Nauvoo across rough and unknown territory. Brigham Young had to organise the movement of over 15 000 people of all ages across this land which was unpredictable both in its geography and climate. Moreover, the Illinois settlers did not allow the Mormons time to finish preparing for their journey During the winter of 1845 every house in Nauvoo was turned into a workshop for the production of wagons and other travelling gear. But in spring 1846, mobs began looting their homes and many Mormons had to leave Nauvoo with their equipment incomplete. Despite this, however, the journey was in other respects well planned, as the following extract from the Church High Council Circular shows:

SOURCE 45

In . . . March a company of pioneers [will set out] consisting mostly of young, hardy men with some families. They are destined to be furnished with an ample outfit; taking with them a printing press, farming utensils of all kinds, with mill irons, seeds of all kinds, grain etc. The object of this early move is to put in a spring crop, to build houses, and to prepare for the reception of families who will start as soon as the grass shall be sufficiently grown to sustain teams and stock.

Mackay, *The Mormons or Latter Day Saints*

The rest of the Mormons then set off by stages in small groups, each harvesting crops planted by the previous group. By the autumn of 1846, several thousands had travelled nearly 650 kilometres to Winter Quarters, a resting station on the west bank of the Missouri River.

Misery Bottom

Many of the Saints suffered severely either during or at the end of this part of the journey. The two extracts below describe some of the problems they faced. Colonel Thomas L. Kane, a US army officer, gave medical aid to some of the Mormons. He described conditions in one of their camps:

ABOVE: The exodus from Nauvoo

SOURCE 46 Colonel Kane's account

The climate of the entire upper 'Misery Bottom', is, during a considerable part of summer and autumn, singularly pestiferous. . . . The Mormons were scourged severely . . . The fever prevailed to such an extent that hardly any escaped from it. They let their cows go unmilked. They wanted for voices to raise the psalms on Sundays. The few who were able to keep their feet, went about among the tents and waggons with food and water. Here at one time the digging got behind hand; burials were slow, and you might see women sit in the open tents keeping the flies off their dead children, some time after decomposition had set in.

O. O. Winter (ed.), *Thomas L. Kane, A Friend of the Mormons*, San Francisco, California, 1937

Difficulties on the journey

One of the Mormon emigrants has left an account of some of their difficulties on the march.

SOURCE 47

We were poorly prepared for such an exodus, and many joining us had but little or nothing of the necessaries for their own sustenance, so our meagre rations had to be divided among them. We had many weeks of cold stormy weather, and our teams being insufficient to draw the loads, made travelling over those soft prairies next thing to an impossibility. Expecting, as we did, to go over the Mountains that year, we were put on rations. During that time our sea biscuits, parched corn meal etc. moulded. Finally they were fed to our horses and cattle.

ABOVE: On the march

At this period the young, and even aged people were forced to walk a goodly portion of the way to save the teams. No matter what the weather might be, storms or excessive heat, or how weary and footsore they became, there was no alternative but to endure till they had reached the spot called Garden Grove.

Rulon S. Howells, *The Mormon Story*, Bookcraft, Salt Lake City, 1962, pp. 1-2

Military discipline

During that first winter Brigham Young taught his followers the secrets of plains travel. He divided them into groups of a hundred with a captain in charge of each. He showed them how to drive their wagons in parallel columns and how to form a circle at night. By the spring, the Mormons were as organised and well disciplined as any army. The advance party led by Brigham Young left Winter Quarters in April 1847. Others followed in stages as on the first part of the journey. From the first a rigid discipline was enforced on all these groups, for the sake of their welfare and safety. They had to be orderly and well organised both in camp and on the march, as the following source shows.

SOURCE 48 An extract from Brigham Young's orders for the journey from William Clayton's journal

At 5.00 in the morning the bugle is to be sounded as a signal for every man to arise and

ABOVE: A Mormon camp

attend prayers before he leaves his wagon. Then cooking, eating, feeding teams etc. till seven o'clock, at which time the camp is to move at the sound of the bugle. Each teamster to keep beside his team, with his loaded gun in his hands. No man to be permitted to leave his wagon unless he obtains permission from his officer. In case of an attack from Indians, the wagons to travel in double file. The order of encampment to be in a circle with the mouth of the wagon to the outside, and the horses and stock tied inside the circle. At 8.30 p.m. the bugle to be sounded again at which time all to have prayers in their wagons and to retire to rest by nine o'clock.

William Clayton, *A Daily Record of the Journey of the Original Company of 'Mormon Pioneers' from Nauvoo to the Valley of the Great Salt Lake*, Salt Lake City, 1921

California or the Great Salt Lake?

Along the route to the Great Salt Lake Basin, Brigham Young and the advance party met three people who warned them against trying to settle there. One of them, Jim Bridger, an old mountain man and trapper, advised them to go to Oregon, as Henry Bigler recalled in his diary.

SOURCE 49

So little faith had Mr. Bridger that he told some of our people, that he would give a thousand dollars for the first bushel of corn raised in this valley.

Elwin Gudde (ed.), *Bigler's Chronicle of the West*, University of California Press, 1962, p. 14

Another trapper gave them similar advice.

SOURCE 50

Mr. Harris says he is well acquainted with the Bear River Valley and the region around the Salt Lake. From his description which is very discouraging, we have little chance to hope for moderately good country anywhere in those regions. He speaks of the whole region being sandy, and destitute of timber and vegetation except the wild sage.

Clayton, *Daily Record of the Journey*

The third man, Sam Brannan, was a Mormon who had sailed round Cape Horn to San Francisco. He had travelled east from California to meet Brigham Young. Brannan gave a 'gloomy account of the Great Salt Lake and the country with its surroundings' and tried to persuade Brigham Young to settle in California. 'For heaven's sake,' Brannan is reported to have said, 'Don't stop in the God forsaken land. Nobody on earth wants it. Come on to California, to a land of sunshine and flowers.' 'Brannan,' Young is said to have replied, 'if there is a place on this earth that nobody wants, that's the place I'm looking for.'

Young knew that if both Oregon and California were so attractive to settlers, then they would not long provide a safe home for the Mormons.

During the journey, Young often talked about how he had seen the Promised Land. 'I will show you when we come to it', he explained.

First impressions of Salt Lake City

Finally, on 22 June 1847, Brigham Young's party reached a place on Big Mountain which looked out on to the Great Salt Lake Valley. According to Mormon

BELOW: First view of the Great Salt Lake

ABOVE: Crossing the Platte River

tradition, Young turned to his companions and said, 'This is the place which the Lord has chosen for us to commence our settlements, and from this place we shall spread abroad and possess the land' (*Journal of Discourses*, XVI, p. 207). William Clayton, another member of Brigham Young's group, recorded his first thoughts as he looked down on the site of his new home.

SOURCE 51

There is an extensive, beautiful, level looking valley from here to the lake. . . . There is but little timber in sight anywhere . . . which is about the only objection which could be raised. There is no prospect for building log houses, but we can make Spanish bricks and dry them in the sun. For my own part I am happily disappointed in the appearance of the valley of the Salt Lake, but if the land be as rich as it has the appearance of being, I have no fear but the Saints can live here and do well. . . . When I ask myself whether I, though poor, would choose to dwell here in this wild looking country amongst the Saints, though poor, or to dwell amongst the gentiles with all their wealth, to be eternally mobbed, harrassed, hunted . . . the soft whisper echoes loud! Give me the quiet wilderness and my family to associate with . . . and adieu to the gentile world.

Clayton, *Daily Record of the Journey*

One of the women in the party, however, later confided to her diary that she was 'heartsick' when she looked upon the valley. 'Weak and weary as I am', she wrote, 'I would rather go a thousand miles farther than remain in such a desolate and forsaken spot as this.'

How to make a way of life in the wilderness?

Brigham Young was sure that the Salt Lake was indeed 'the place' for the Mormons simply because it was such 'a desolate and forsaken spot'. But his decision to settle in this valley did not mean an end to the Mormons' problems. They still had to find some way of living in this dry and treeless valley. How were they going to provide enough homes and food not only for themselves, but also for the thousands of Saints who were already on their way to the Salt Lake basin?

'This land is beautifully situated for irrigation'

The growing of food in such a dry valley was the first problem to be faced. The advance party realised at once that the soil was fertile, all it needed was water. It was obvious that the rainfall would never be sufficient to water crops. Their only hope, therefore, was to irrigate the land in the valley using water from the mountain streams. Within a day of their arrival they had made a start.

SOURCE 52

Friday 23rd As soon as the camp was formed, . . . the brethren immediately rigged three plows and set to plowing a little northeast of the camp; another party went with the spades etc. to make a dam on one of the creeks so as to throw the water on the field, designing to irrigate the land. . . . This land is beautifully situated for irrigation. . . .

Saturday 24th Many are gone to planting potatoes. Others are still at work on the dams. . . . There appears to be a unanimous agreement in regard to the richness of the soil and there are good prospects of fattening stock. The only objection is a lack of timber and rain.

Clayton, *Daily Record of the Journey*, p. 31

It was now clear to Brigham Young that irrigated farming land would be vital to the survival of the Saints in the valley. He also knew that he must make sure that everyone had a fair share of both land and water. There must be no quarrelling or ill-feeling about such an important matter. At his next meeting with the advance party, therefore, he announced the principle that was to decide how all land and water in the valley was to be distributed.

SOURCE 53

No man can ever buy land here, for no one has any land to sell. But every man shall have

his land measured out to him, which he must cultivate in order to keep it.

Besides, there shall be no private ownership of the streams that come out of the canyons, nor the timber that grows on the hills. These belong to the people; all the people.

R. A. Billington, *Westward Expansion*, Macmillan, 1967, p. 540

ABOVE: Salt Lake City in 1873

As more settlers arrived committees were set up to plan and dig a network of irrigation channels. The use of water from these channels was strictly controlled. No farmer was allowed to take more than he needed.

'The average life . . . is a hard one'

Despite all the hard work and planning, an irrigation system could not be constructed in a short time. In 1847 the Saints' first harvest was badly affected by drought and food supplies ran short that winter.

The following year their harvest was a little better. But in the early years it was never easy to make a living in the valley. Horace Greeley, a New York journalist, visited the valley in 1859 and described the problems the Mormons still faced ten years later.

SOURCE 54

The gardens are well filled with peach, apple and other fruit trees. Apricots and grapes are grown though not yet abundant; so of strawberries. Plums are in profusion, and the mountain currants are large, abundant and very good.

Still the average life in Utah is a hard one. The climate is severe and capricious—now intensely hot and dry, in winter cold and stormy; and though cattle are usually allowed to shift for themselves in the valleys, they are apt to resent the insult by dying. Crickets and grasshoppers swarm in myriads, and often devour all before them. Wood is scarce and poor. Irrigation is laborious and expensive; as yet, it has not been found practicable to irrigate one-fourth of the arable land at all. Frost is very destructive here; Indian corn rarely escapes it wholly and wheat often suffers from it. I estimate that 159 days' faithful labor in Kansas will produce as many of the necessities of life as 300 such days' work in Utah. Hence, the adults here generally wear a toil-worn, anxious look, and many of them are older in frame than in years.

Greeley, *New York to San Francisco, 1859*, pp. 200-1

The building of Salt Lake City

The building of homes for the thousands of Saints was also a problem which had to be solved. As soon as Brigham Young had announced the principle that the land belonged to all the people', committees of Church Leaders were appointed to begin marking out a city. In the centre a large square was reserved for public buildings including a temple and meeting place. Around these the streets and housing plots were arranged in a regular plan. In 1850, Captain Howard Stansbury, a member of

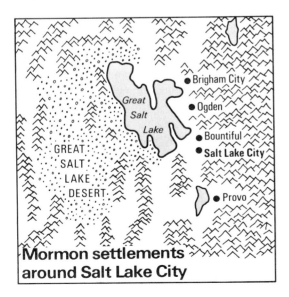

Mormon settlements around Salt Lake City

the US Topographical Engineers, made a survey of the valley for the US government. He wrote this description of the city:

SOURCE 55

A city has been laid out upon a magnificent scale. . . . Through the city itself flows an unfailing stream of pure, sweet water, which, by an ingenious mode of irrigation, is made to traverse each side of every street whence it is led into every garden-spot, spreading life, and beauty over what was heretofore a barren waste. . . .

The houses are built, principally, of adobe, or sun-dried brick, which . . . make a warm, comfortable dwelling, presenting a very neat appearance.

H. Stansbury, *An Expedition to the Valley of the Great Salt Lake of Utah*, Philadelphia, 1855, p. 128

ABOVE: The Temple, Tabernacle and Assembly Hall, Salt Lake City

'Let the sisters think of what they can wear that is Zion made'

Within two or three years the Mormons had shown that they could survive in the Salt Lake Valley. But survival was not enough. They also had to make themselves as independent as possible from the outside world. This meant that they had to produce not only their own food, but also their own clothes and manufactured goods.

But as with their irrigation schemes, things were never easy for the Mormons. Horace Greeley, the New York journalist, describes the problems they still faced in 1859:

SOURCE 56

Up to this hour, the Mormons' manufacturing energies have been most unhappily directed. Some two hundred thousand dollars was expended in preparations for iron-making at a place called Cedar City; but the ore, though rich, would not flux, and the enterprise had to be totally abandoned. Wood and flax can be grown here cheaply and abundantly, yet, owing to the troubles last year, no spinning and weaving machinery has yet been put in operation. An attempt to grow cotton is likely to prove a failure. The winters are long and cold here, and the Saints must make cloth or shiver.

Sugar is another necessary of life which they have had bad luck with. They can grow the beet very well, but it is said to yield little or no sugar—because, it is supposed, of an excess of alkali in the soil.

Greeley, *New York to San Francisco, 1859*, p. 198

LEFT: The Pioneer Ore Crushing Mill

'We feel the need of more labourers'

If the Mormons were to become totally independent of the outside world more people would be needed to work on the farms and in the factories. Brigham Young made this very clear in his 'Second General Epistle . . . to the Saints scattered throughout the Earth':

SOURCE 57

We feel the need of more labourers, for more efficient help, and multiplied means of farming and building at this place. We want men, Brethren, come from the States, from the Nations, come! and help us to build and grow, until we can say, enough—the valleys of Ephraim are full. Any of the brethren, master workmen in cotton or woollen factories, who will come on with their means, machinery and hands to work it, will meet a warm reception.

Millenial Star, Liverpool, 1850

A Perpetual Emigration Fund was set up to provide money to help poor converts from the United States and Europe to come to Salt Lake City. Between 1856 and 1860 when the fund was short of money, Brigham Young directed thousands of converts to walk across America to Salt Lake City pulling their possessions in hand carts. Thousands perished, but the number of Mormons in the Salt Lake Valley steadily increased. In time, other settlements were started around Salt Lake City.

Brigham Young and the State of Deseret

The schemes for building factories and attracting more converts were only part of Brigham Young's plan for making the Saints independent of the outside world. He was also determined to ensure that the Saints would remain free to worship as they wished and to practise polygamy. Brigham Young believed that the only way to guarantee this freedom was for the Mormons to govern themselves.

In 1847 when the Mormons had first arrived in Salt Lake Valley, they confidently expected that they would be allowed to govern themselves. They had settled in an isolated corner of Mexican territory and hoped to be able to reach some arrangement with the Mexican government.

Then, in 1848, only one year after their arrival in the valley, the Mormons received most alarming news. After a short war between the United States and Mexico, the United States government had been granted possession of a vast area of Mexican territory in the southern Rockies, including the Salt Lake Valley. Brigham Young decided immediately that only one thing could now protect the Mormons.

LEFT: Hand cart emigrants in a storm

expressed. The US government refused to agree to the Mormons' request for independence. Instead the area became a 'Territory' of the United States. It was to be known as the Territory of Utah after the Ute Indians who lived in this area.

They must apply to be admitted into the Union as an independent Mormon state with their own laws, religion and government. In October 1849 Brigham Young made the following announcement in his 'Second General Epistle to the Saints':

SOURCE 58

The inhabitants of this great Basin have instituted a provisional state of government, adopted a constitution, elected officers, and we anticipate that at the next session of Congress, we shall be admitted into the Union, free and independent like our sister states. We call our new state, Deseret [meaning, 'the land of the honey-bee'].

Mulder and Mortensen, *Amongst the Mormons*, p. 228

Outcry in the East
This news caused great alarm in the eastern states. Once again all the old hatred and fear of the Mormons, especially of their polygamy, began to be loudly

Although the US government appointed Brigham Young as the Governor, the Mormons were not allowed to pass their own laws. The law and many other aspects of life were to be administered by US government officials and judges.

The next seven years were a time of great tension between the Mormons and the US government. The government was faced with the constant complaints of judges in Utah against the Mormons. 'Mormons look to Brigham Young and to him alone for the law by which they are governed', one irate judge reported. Public opinion in the East became even more violently anti-Mormon as reports came in of Brigham Young's ruthless dictatorship and his use of the Danites or 'destroying angels' to crush all opposition. Government officials were 'constantly insulted, harassed and annoyed'. Some were killed.

Crisis in Utah
In 1857, matters reached a crisis point. The US government decided to send a non-Mormon Governor to Salt Lake City, together with a detachment of 1500 troops to see that the United States law was enforced.

LEFT: *Uncle Sam's abscess* anti-Mormon tract written in 1884

Fear of 'invasion' raised tempers in Salt Lake City to fever pitch. In September 1857, 140 emigrants from a wagon train, many of them hated Missourians, were massacred at Mountain Meadows (see map, p. 49). The Mormons blamed the Indians, but the Gentiles blamed the Danites. Whatever the truth of the matter, the Mountain Meadows massacre had a great impact. The US government realised that much bloodshed would follow an encounter between the Mormon legions and federal troops. They decided to seek a peaceful settlement. Colonel Thomas L. Kane, a supporter of the Mormons, was sent to negotiate. Even so, when troops finally entered Salt Lake City in June 1858, they found it deserted. The Saints had packed their belongings and were prepared to move yet again.

'Brigham Young is King'

After skilful negotiations, however, an agreement was reached and the Mormons returned to Salt Lake City. The federal government assured the Mormons that they had no wish to interfere with their religion. In return the Mormons agreed to accept a 'Gentile' governor. The US government continued to refuse to allow Utah to become a state until polygamy was officially forbidden by the Mormon Church in 1890. Nevertheless from the 1860s the Mormons were allowed to develop their own way of life in the Salt Lake Valley. As one traveller explained 'There is a batch of governors and judges and other officials here shipped from Washington but . . . Brigham Young is King'.

Many Gentiles and Mormon apostates preferred to put it another way and said that Utah was a police state.

In 1861 President Lincoln explained the new US government policy to a Mormon representative in Washington.

SOURCE 59

When I was a boy on the farm in Illinois, there was a great deal of timber which we had to clear away. Occasionally, we would come to a log which . . . was too hard to split, too wet to burn and too heavy to move, so we plowed around it. That's what I intend to do with the Mormons.

Huston Horn, *The Pioneers*, p. 181

This was not what the Mormons had hoped for when they first came to the Salt Lake Valley. But eventually they came to accept that total isolation was impossible. To be 'plowed around' and left to live their own lives was enough.

LEFT: United States troops entering Salt Lake City

LEFT: 'Hail to the Chief!' 'The Lion of the Lord': Mormons with banners greet Brigham Young
ABOVE: A cartoon depicting the widows of Brigham Young

3
Cowboys and cattlemen

White settlers on the Great Plains

By 1860 American settlers were firmly established in many different areas of the Far West including California, the Salt Lake Basin and the mining regions of the Rocky Mountains. However, with the exception of the Texans in the river valley of the south and the traders along the trails, no white men had yet chosen to settle out on the Great Plains. The myth still persisted that the plains were a desert, and travellers on the trails in the 1840s and 1850s saw only a vast landscape with little but 'cows [buffalo] and sky', wild game and Plains Indians.

A traveller who crossed the plains in 1890, however, would have seen a different landscape. Where buffalo and Indians once roamed he would have seen fields of corn, threshing machines and homesteads. Further west, cattle, ranch houses and cowboys on horseback were a more familiar sight. How did this change come about? When and why did these white settlers decide that they could, after all, make a life on the plains? Let us look at first at the cattlemen (or cattle ranchers) and their hired hands, the cowboys.

The cattlemen were able to build their lives around the three natural products of the plains: wild cattle, wild horses and grass. Like the Indians before them they learnt to live there by adapting themselves to the Great Plains. The cattlemen and the cowboys were important because they were the first people effectively to explode the myth of the Great American Desert. Instead it became known as the 'Cattle Kingdom'. It took the farmers longer to come to terms with conditions out on the High Plains, as we shall see later.

ABOVE: Longhorn cattle from Texas
OPPOSITE: A trail boss watching his herd being watered

To find the origins of the Cattle Kingdom, we must look at Texas, for it was there that the four basic components of ranching first came together: the cattle, the horses, the grass and the men.

The beginning of the Cattle Kingdom in Texas

The Spanish vaqueros

The first cattle owners and cowboys were the Spaniards. They brought cattle as well as horses with them from Spain to the New World in the sixteenth century. By the eighteenth century they had conquered the whole of Mexico, California and Texas in the south western corner of North America. In time, Spanish settlers began cattle ranching in Texas. Most of these ranches were in the triangle of land

between the Nueces River, the Rio Grande and the Gulf of Mexico (see map, p. 65).

The Texas ranches were run on the same lines as those in Mexico. Since there were no fences, cattle were allowed to wander freely on the open range to graze and breed. Because the cattle from different herds intermingled, a system of branding was developed so that the owners could identify their own cattle by a distinguishing mark. And, because the cattle wandered over a large area, men on horseback had to be employed to round them up. The Mexican cowmen were called vaqueros (from the Spanish *vaca*, a cow) and they were the ancestors of the American cowboys. Besides the cattle from the ranches, there were also a great number of wild cattle. These were descendants of cattle originally brought from Spain and lost or left behind by the first Spanish explorers.

This, then, was the state of cattle ranching in Texas when the first Americans were allowed to settle there by the Mexican government in the 1820s. The American settlers, however, were farmers and cattle ranching was at first not important to them. Then in 1836 the Texans rebelled against the Mexican government and established their own independent republic. For a time the Mexican ranchers stayed but they were increasingly harassed by Texan cattle raiders. Eventually the Mexican ranchers abandoned their land and many of their

BELOW: Spanish vaqueros on a ranch in California

ABOVE: Roping a Longhorn

cattle and retreated to safety over the Rio Grande.

Texas ranchers

The Texans soon moved into the area and found hundreds of cattle roaming free on the open range. They began to round up the herds and brand them with their own marks. They also adopted the methods, dress and equipment used by Mexican vaqueros. Between 1838 and 1860 the cattle herds increased and a few Texans began setting up their own cattle ranches in the Nueces Valley. Even at this time, however, most Texans still did not take ranching very seriously. The cattle were plentiful and free but there was no market for beef near enough to make sales profitable.

In 1861 the Civil War broke out. Many Texas cattlemen left their farms and ranches and went off to fight in the Southern army. For four years many ranchers were absent. In the meantime, the cattle continued to breed and to grow even wilder. Because of their uncertain life on the open range these Texas Longhorns became tougher and sturdier. When compared to modern cattle they gave little beef and milk, but they had developed a remarkable ability to survive shortages of food and water and extremes of temperature. Their hardiness became their most valued quality in the years which followed.

The beginning of the 'Long Drive'

Charles Goodnight: Cowman and Plainsman

The story of Charles Goodnight is typical of the many Texans who began cattle ranching in the days just before the Civil War. As a child in 1845 he came to Texas with his family to farm on the Brazos River. There, like many other young men, he quickly learned how to rope and catch wild horses and cattle. In 1856 Goodnight and his step-brother went into the cattle business. They took care of 430 cattle from the neighbouring CV ranch. As pay they were allowed to keep every fourth calf. By 1860 they had 180 cattle of their own. Then in the following year came the Civil War, and Goodnight joined the Texas Rangers.

When Charles Goodnight and his fellow-soldiers returned home at the end of the war they found Texas in a poor state. Their farms and ranches were run down. Confederate (Southern) money was value-less. Goodnight and his neighbour soon realised that their only asset was their cattle. When Goodnight and his step-brother finally rounded up their portion of the CV herd they found it had increased in their absence to about 5000 head of cattle. Other cattlemen found the same: by the end of the Civil War it has been estimated that some five million Long-horns were roaming the ranges of Texas.

ABOVE: Charles Goodnight
ABOVE RIGHT: On the 'Long Drive'

But these cattle were worth little unless buyers could be found for them.

Then, word began to get around that the end of the war had brought a shortage of beef in the big cities of the north, such as Chicago. Buyers in the Chicago meat markets were prepared to pay $30 to $40 a head for cattle—ten times their value in Texas. Similarly high prices for beef were also to be had in other markets in the mining towns of the North West. Charles Goodnight and his fellow Texans knew that somehow, if they were to recover from the war, they would have to get their cattle to the markets.

Throughout the winter of 1865-6 the Texas cattlemen were busily rounding up Longhorns, building wagons and hiring cowboys. By the spring of 1866 Charles Goodnight had increased his herd to 8000. As soon as the grass began to grow the cattlemen started to drive their herds north on the hoof to new markets. The first of the 'long drives' had begun. That year two main trails were followed. Most of the cattlemen drove their herds north-east to the rail head at Sedalia. There the cattle could be loaded on to trains for shipment east to St Louis and then on to Chicago (see map, p. 65).

Charles Goodnight, however, decided to try his luck in the other direction and to open up a new route to the mining towns and army forts of Colorado. In June 1866 Goodnight and his new partner Oliver Loving gathered together 2000 Longhorns and eighteen cowboys. At the end of the

summer the entire herd was sold at a fine profit. Goodnight sold one half to the US government's Indian agents for the reservations of the Navahos and Apaches. Oliver Loving drove the other half on to the mining town of Denver and sold them to a man named John Iliffe. We shall hear more about him later. That autumn Goodnight headed back down the trail with a mule carrying $12 000 in gold in its pack-saddles.

Problems on the first long drive

The long drive had certainly proved worth while for Charles Goodnight and other Texans. But both trails also proved to have many dangers. Goodnight and Oliver Loving faced problems from lack of water and Indian attacks. Cowboys on the Sedalia trail were attacked by angry farmers who feared that the Longhorns would bring Texas cattle fever. They were also harassed by robbers and cattle rustlers. The problem of Indian attacks on the Goodnight-Loving trail was not solved for another fifteen years. In fact, the following year Oliver Loving died from a wound received in a Comanche attack. Cattlemen on the Sedalia trail, however, did manage to find a safer route.

Abilene, first of the Cow Towns

Their problem was solved in the spring of 1867 by Joseph McCoy, an Illinois cattle dealer. He had heard of the difficulties faced by the cowboys in 1866 and was convinced that a place must be found where southern cattlemen and northern buyers could meet and trade in safety. The spot he chose for this meeting place was Abilene on the Kansas Pacific Railroad. In 1867 Abilene was in McCoy's words 'a small, dead place . . . of about one dozen log huts'—and in the middle of nowhere! But it had all he wanted. On 5 September the first cattle were shipped from Abilene to Chicago, and by the end of the year 35 000 had made their way east from McCoy's stockyards (source 60).

As the railway line was built further west more cow towns were set up, such as Dodge City, Ellsworth and Wichita. New trails were laid heading for these towns and each in its turn had its hey-day and became the centre of trade (source 61).

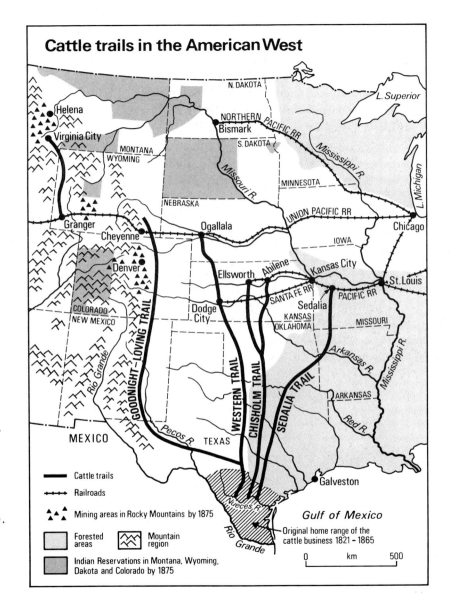

Cattle trails in the American West

Legend:
- ▬▬ Cattle trails
- ┼┼┼ Railroads
- ▲▲▲ Mining areas in Rocky Mountains by 1875
- Forested areas
- ⋀⋀ Mountain region
- Indian Reservations in Montana, Wyoming, Dakota and Colorado by 1875
- Original home range of the cattle business 1821–1865

0 km 500

SOURCE 60 Joseph McCoy's description of the opening of Abilene as a cattle market in 1867

Abilene was selected because the country was entirely unsettled, well watered, had excellent grass, and nearly the entire area of country was adapted to holding cattle. And it was the farthest point east at which a good depot for cattle business could have been made. After the point had been decided on, the labour of getting material upon the ground began. In sixty days from July 1st a shipping yard that would accommodate three thousand cattle, a large pair of Fairbank's scales, a barn and an office were completed, and a good three storey hotel well on the way toward completion. A man was sent into Southern Kansas and Indian Territory to tell [the cowboys and cattlemen] of Abilene.

The first herd that arrived at Abilene was driven from Texas. About 35 000 head were driven in 1867. Great hardships attended driving that year on account of Osage Indian troubles, excessive rainstorms and flooded rivers and but little of the first year's arrivals were fit to go to market. However, on the 5th September, 1867 the first shipment of twenty [rail] cars was made to Chicago. This train of cattle sold in Chicago to a speculator at a small profit to the shipper. Texan cattle beef was not then considered eatable, and was as unsaleable in the Eastern markets as a shipment of prairie wolves. But consumers soon learned that well fatted Texas beef was as good as any other kind and much cheaper.

Joseph McCoy, *Historic Sketches of the Cattle Trade of the West and South West*, Kansas City, Missouri, pp. 50-3

SOURCE 61 Texas cattle drives 1866-1880

Place and year	Head of cattle
To Sedalia	
1866	260 000
To Abilene	
1867	35 000
1868	75 000
1869	350 000
1870	300 000
1871	700 000
To Wichita and Ellsworth	
1872	350 000
1873	405 000
1874	166 000
1875	151 618
To Dodge City and Ellis	
1876	322 000
1877	201 159
1878	265 646
1879	257 927

Tenth Census of the United States, 1880

The spread of cattle ranching to the northern plains

For the next four years, despite the hazards of his western trail, Charles Goodnight continued to drive herd after herd to Colorado. It was during these journeys that he came to realise that Texas was not the only place where cattle could be raised successfully. Colorado too had plenty of grass. In 1870 Goodnight acquired a plot of land on the Arkansas River near Pueblo, Colorado. He was married, built a ranchhouse and became a rancher instead of a cattle drover. He still, however, continued to have cattle trailed up from Texas to stock his range. The yearly arrival of vast herds of Texas Longhorns not only aroused the interest of the

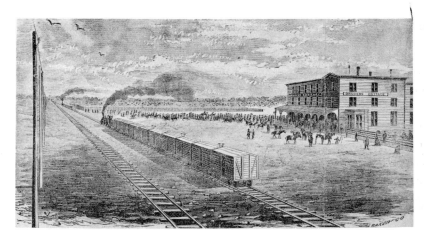

Colorado miners; fairly soon, other people began to follow in Charles Goodnight's footsteps and buy the Texas Longhorns to start their own ranches in the northern plains. By 1880 cattle ranches had been set up over six huge territories in the north of the Great Plains, all stocked with Texas Longhorns (source 62).

ABOVE LEFT: Cattle train leaving Ellsworth, Kansas
ABOVE: Loading cattle at Wichita, Kansas

SOURCE 62 The growth of the cattle industry in the northern plains

State/territory	Cattle in 1860	Cattle in 1880
Kansas	93 455	1 533 133
Nebraska	37 197	1 113 247
Colorado	none	791 492
Wyoming	none	521 213
Montana	none	428 279
Dakota	none	140 815

Tenth Census of the United States, 1880

BELOW: The Union Stockyards, Chicago, 1860

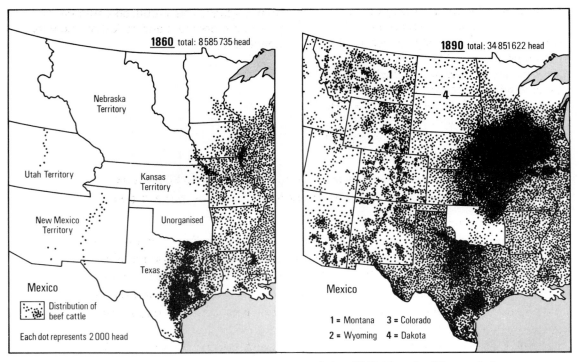

1860 total: 8 585 735 head

Nebraska
Territory

Utah Territory

New Mexico
Territory

Kansas
Territory

Unorganised

Texas

Mexico

☐ Distribution of
beef cattle

Each dot represents 2 000 head

1890 total: 34 851 622 head

1
4
2
3

Mexico

1 = Montana   3 = Colorado
2 = Wyoming   4 = Dakota

The spread of cattle ranching over the Great Plains 1860-1890

John Iliff 'Cattle King of the northern plains'

John Wesley Iliff was typical of one of these northern cattlemen. He had bought part of Goodnight and Loving's first herd in 1866. Iliff was born in 1831, the son of an Ohio farmer. At the age of twenty-five he was attracted by stories of the pioneer life in the West. So he left home and set up in business in Kansas as a trader, selling stores to the emigrants on the California and Oregon trails. In 1859 news came of gold discoveries near Pikes Peak in Colorado. Iliff moved out along the trail to Colorado to catch the new trade from the miners. The following year Iliff, like many other small traders, also began to graze a few cattle.

Iliff soon realised that as grass was free, he could make more money by grazing cattle than by trading. In 1861 he became a full-time rancher. But where could he get more cattle from? It would take years to build up a herd by relying on 'footsores' from the wagon trains. Then in 1866 he heard of the arrival in Colorado of Oliver Loving and his Texas Longhorns. Iliff bought all the cattle. Within a few years traders all over the northern plains were following his example.

The arrival of the Texas cattlemen and their Longhorns could not have come at a better time. In 1867 the Union Pacific Railway construction gangs set up camp near Cheyenne. Iliff arranged to supply the gangs (and troops who came to guard them against Indian attacks) with beef (source 63). By the end of 1868 the railway was built as far as Cheyenne and Iliff was able to sell even more beef— this time to the eastern cities. Some of his cattle were slaughtered and shipped in iced railroad cars to dealers in Chicago.

ABOVE: John Iliff

In 1868 Red Cloud and many of his Sioux moved to a reservation and Iliff won a contract to supply this reservation with beef (source 64). From this time on, Iliff's business grew and flourished (source 65). In addition to buying more and more cattle from Texas (source 66), he began to cross breed his Longhorns with Durham and Hereford bulls imported from England. This produced cattle which provided more meat and milk than the wiry Longhorns.

SOURCE 63 Advertisement in the 'Rocky Mountain News', 20 September 1869, for a beef contract which was awarded to Iliff at $6.90 per 100 pounds

Notice to Contractors

Sealed proposals will be received at the offices of Evans and Carr, First National Bank Building, Denver, until Monday 12M [mid-day], September 20th for furnishing delivered at any station on the Denver Pacific Railway, the beef, flour, potatoes, cabbage, turnips, onions, oats, corn and hay required by the track laying forces during the construction of the said road. Responsible guarantees must accompany bids. Payments will be made monthly:—John Evans.

Frink, Jackson and Spring, *When Grass was King*, University of Colorado Press, 1956, pp. 562-3

SOURCE 64 Extract from a letter written 20 February 1872 by J. W. Wham, Indian Agent for the Red Cloud Reservation, to Indian Affairs Commissioner at Washington

On taking charge of the Red Cloud Indians at Fort Laramie, I saw their allowance of beef was insufficient for their subsistence if kept at an Agency where they could not keep game. I asked therefore, the Department of the Interior for authority to increase the ration when necessary. In the meantime the Indians were clamouring for more beef. And threatening to leave the Agency and go where they could get game if I could not increase the ration. There were then at the Post upwards of 7000 Indians who were daily becoming dissatisfied.

'Records of the Red Cloud Agency', Bureau of Indian Affairs, National Archives and Records Service, Washington DC, in Frink, Jackson and Spring, *When Grass was King*, pp. 370-1

ABOVE: Union Pacific Railroad construction gang at work

BELOW: John W. Snyder

SOURCE 65 Extract from a letter by John Iliff in the 'Rocky Mountain News', 3 August 1870

I have been engaged in the stock business in Colorado and Wyoming for the past eight years. During all that time I have grazed stock in nearly all the valleys of these territories, both summer and winter. The cost of both summering and wintering is simply the cost of herding, as no feeding or sheltering is required. I consider the summer cured grasses of these plains and valleys as superior to hay. My cattle have not only kept in good order on the grass through all of the eight winters, but many of them, thin in the fall, have become fine beef by spring. During this time I have owned twenty thousand head of cattle.

Frink, Jackson and Spring, *When Grass was King*, pp. 367-8

SOURCE 66 Extracts from a contract for 15 000 Texas Cattle

These articles of agreement [were] made this 9th day of August 1877 between Dudley and John W. Snyder of Round Rock, Texas and John W. Iliff of Denver, Colorado.

Dudley and John W. Snyder promise to buy 15 000 head of steers of the ages of two and three years next spring, and to drive the cattle to Colorado from Texas and deliver to John Iliff at his Wild Cat or Riverside Ranch in Weld County in July 1878. Upon delivering the steers John Iliff agrees to allow Sixteen Dollars per head for the three year old steers and Twelve Dollars for the two years old per head.

Witness   (signed) *D. H. & J. W. Snyder*

Amos Steck   *J. W. Iliff*

Exhibit B in Document File # 381, Denver County Court; in Frink, Jackson and Spring, *When Grass was King*, pp. 415-7

The spread of ranching throughout Texas

By 1880 ranches had not only been established all over the northern plains, they had also begun to spread over the whole of Texas. The building of railroads into the heart of Texas helped would-be ranchers to make up their minds. Cattlemen no longer had to trail cattle hundreds of kilometres to the railheads at Dodge or Ellsworth. They could now be loaded onto trains much nearer home. Less sturdy but meatier cattle like those being bred on northern ranches could now be introduced into Texas. By 1890 the whole of central and northern Texas had been carved up into enormous ranches.

The ranch and the open range

We have now seen how men like Iliffe and Goodnight set up cattle ranches all over the Great Plains in the fifteen years after the Civil War. But what exactly do we mean when we talk about a ranch? The word 'ranch' can mean two things—

first the ranch house where the cattlemen and cowboys lived. Secondly, it means the open range around the ranch house where cattle grazed.

In the early years of the business the cattlemen, like the Indians, had to be prepared to move their homes to wherever the cattle roamed. In many cases their homes were little more than a sod shanty or a dug-out. When cattle ranching became more of a full time business ranchers began to build more permanent homes. Most provided similar accommodation: the bunkhouse or the living quarters where the ranch owner and his cowboys lived and slept; a cookhouse where they ate and a 'dog trot' or covered way which joined the two separate buildings.

The cattlemen may have owned their ranch houses, but few owned the land on

ABOVE: Cattle grazing on the open range
LEFT: Railroad advertisement

BELOW: A ranch house in Wyoming in the 1880s

which the house stood. No one at first owned the land on which the cattle grazed. It was public domain—the open range—free for all to use. Many cattlemen had no wish to own their own land. All they needed was cattle, grass and water and all these were free. Hundreds of hectares were needed to graze a herd of cattle in an area of such scanty rainfall. The average ranch on the Great Plains, therefore, covered 80 to 100 square km. No cattleman could afford to buy so much land. Each cattleman did however have his own equivalent of the Indians' hunting grounds—these were his 'range rights'. He was allowed by custom (but not by law) to reserve for his cattle a stream or watering place and the land running back behind it as far as the next 'divide' or highland which separated his watering place from the next one.

Sharp-witted cattlemen like Goodnight and Iliffe realised that by buying or home-steading (see below left) a little area of land along the rivers they could actually gain control of most of the land behind. Without water, land was no use to anyone else. Each cattleman knew where his own range rights began and ended—but since there were no fences these meant little to the cattle. They wandered freely on the open range in search of food. It was the brand mark and not a fence which told the rancher which cattle were his. The rounding up, branding and care of these wandering herds was too much for one man and this is why the ranchers hired the help of the cowboys.

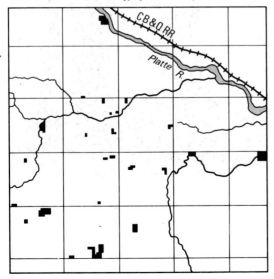

BELOW: Map showing areas of land owned or controlled by the Swan Cattle Company in Laramie County, Wyoming. Ownership of this small area of land (brown) enabled them to control most of the range (white area)

The life of the cowboy

SOURCE 67 The Virginian

Lounging there at ease against the wall was a slim young giant more beautiful than pictures. His broad soft hat was pushed back, a loose knotted dull-scarlet handkerchief sagged from his throat, and one casual thumb was hooked in the cartridge belt that slanted across his hips. He had plainly come from somewhere across the vast horizon as the dust upon him showed. His boots were white with it. The weather beaten bloom of his face shone through it duskily like ripe peaches. But no dinginess could tarnish the splendour [of] his youth and strength. Had I been the bride I would have taken the giant, dust and all.

Owen Wister, *The Virginian*, Pocket Books, 1956, p. 3

This is Owen Wister's description of The Virginian. He is one of the most famous of fictional cowboys. Now compare him with the picture of a real cowboy. How do they differ? How true a picture of the cowboy life do we get from films on TV and the cinema? The writer of a book on Roy Rogers, a film cowboy of the 1950s, described his life as one of excitement and adventure. David Shirk, a real cowboy of the 1860s, had a different view; he called it 'that sleepless grind—that never ending vigil of weary days and sleepless nights'.

Below you will see a number of extracts and pictures which provide a description of cowboy life as it really was. They show that the cowboy's life was in some ways similar to that of the Indian. The Indian centred his life around the buffalo. The cowboy centred his around the movements and needs of the Longhorns. Throughout the winter and early spring cowboys had to look after the cattle on the open range. In late spring the cattle had to be rounded up and branded. In the summer, the sale cattle had to be driven to the railheads. Study these sources carefully and then complete a diary of a year in a cowboy's life.

ABOVE: Nat Love, a Negro cowboy

SOURCE 68 Who were the cowboys?

Nor were all cowboys all . . . Anglo-Saxon types popularized by the film maker. Not unnaturally, a good many of them were negroes. When the cattle drives began, some 182 000 ex-slaves lived in Texas. Many of them accustomed to life in the saddle . . . they would logically be hired as drovers . . . as would other negroes who moved westward after the Civil War to escape eastern discrimination.

Billington, *Westward Expansion*, p. 593

The cowboy's outfit

SOURCE 69 The cowboy's outfit as described by Everett Dick, one of the first historians of cowboys and cattle ranching

The dress of the cowboy was picturesque and distinctive. It was, however, not worn with the view of producing an effect but rather for comfort and convenience.

The hat was made of felt. The broad brim protected the wearer from the sun and was an umbrella in rainy weather. In winter it could be pulled down over the ears and tied thus giving protection from frostbite. It was used to fan the campfires; swung

ABOVE: Trail boss on a cattle drive in Montana in the 1880s

in the air [it was] a means for signalling. It might be folded and used for a pillow. These hats were usually called 'stetsons' after the Philadelphia manufacturer who practically monopolised the trade.

The bandana. The handkerchief (usually a red bandana) which was worn around the neck was intended for use as a mask. When the cowboy rode along behind the herd of cattle, he pulled the handkerchief up over his nose and mouth protecting himself from the cloud of alkaline dust.

The 'chaps' were an overgarment [like] a pair of trousers [with] a cut-out seat. Many were made of the shaggy skin of a bear, goat or sheep. Should a horse fall on a man, the fur-faced 'chaps' would protect his leg. They were also to withstand the thorny vegetation. They kept the rider's legs from becoming chafed during a long ride and turned the cutting north wind in winter.

Coat, vest and gloves. The cowboy liked to go coatless whenever possible, but he always wore a vest [waistcoat]. This was usually left unbuttoned. In cold weather and while roping, gloves were usually worn.

Boots and spurs. All cowboys wore high heeled boots. The heel and arch were so constructed that the foot and leg were comfortable when riding. Spurs were worn at all times.

Saddle. The saddle was the cowboy's throne—its bumps and contours grew to fit the owner's body. A man might gamble away his money, horse or chaps, but he would put his saddle on his back and return home on foot.

Everett Dick, 'The Long Drive' in *Collections of the Kansas State Historical Society*, 1926-28, Vol. XVII, pp. 49-53

The winter routine

SOURCE 70 Riding the range in winter described by Theodore Roosevelt who had a cattle ranch on the plains in the 1880s

In the winter there is much less work than at any other season, but what there is involves great hardship and exposure. Many of the men are discharged after the summer is over, and during much of the cold weather, there is little to do except hunt now and then, and on very bitter days lounge listlessly about the house. But some of the men are out in the line camps. . . . The men in the line camps lead a hard life, for they have to be out in every kind of weather, and should be especially active and watchful during the storms. The camps are established along some line which it is proposed to make the boundary of the cattle's drift in a given direction. We strongly object to their drifting, especially as when they drift that way they come out on flat, bare plains where there is danger of perishing.

The camps are usually for two men each, and some fifteen or twenty miles apart; the camp itself is sometimes merely a tent pitched in a sheltered coulée, but ought to be either made of logs or else a dug-out in the ground. A small corral and horse shed is near by. In riding over the beat each man drives any cattle that have come near it back into the Bad Lands, and if he sees by the hoof-marks that a few have strayed out over the line very recently, he will follow and fetch them home.

Theodore Roosevelt, *Ranch Life and the Hunting Trail*, The Century Co., 1899, p. 74

ABOVE: Cowboys at a line camp by Frederic Remington

SOURCE 71 'Bog riding time' described by Theodore Roosevelt

During the early spring months before the round-up begins, the chief work is in hauling out mired cows and steers. As long as everything is frozen solid there is, of course, no danger from miring; but when the thaw comes [and] the frost goes out of the soil, the ground round every little alkali-spring changes into a trembling quagmire, and deep holes of slimy, tenacious mud form in the bottom of all the gullies. The cattle, which have had to live on snow for three or four months, are very eager for water, and are weak and in poor condition. They rush heedlessly into any pool and stand there, drinking gallons of icy water and sinking steadily into the mud.

Roosevelt, *Ranch Life and the Hunting Trail*, p. 28

BELOW: Bringing in a downer

SOURCE 72 Extracts from 'Rules of the X.I.T. Ranch', January 1888

No. 11 No employee of the Company is permitted to carry on or about his person or saddlebags, any pistol, dirk, dagger, sling shot, knuckles, bowie knife or any other similar instruments for the purpose of offence or defence.

No. 12 Card playing and gambling of every description is strictly forbidden on the ranch.

No. 15 Employees are strictly forbidden the use of vinous, malt, spirituous or intoxicating liquors, during their time of service with the Company.

ABOVE: Cowboy pulling a cow out of
the mud by Frederic Remington

No. 20 Loafers, 'sweaters', deadbeats, tramps, gamblers, or disreputable persons, must not be entertained at any camp.

J. Evetts Haley, *X.I.T. Ranch of Texas and the Early Days of the Llano Estacado*, University of Oklahoma Press, 1953, pp. 241-5

The spring round up

SOURCE 73 A round up, described by Reginald Aldridge, an Englishman who was a cattle rancher in Kansas in the 1870s

Let us suppose that we are going to round up [the cattle in] a certain section of the country. Some point is fixed on the river that runs through that section, at which to commence work. Everyone likely to have any cattle in that neighbourhood sends one or more representatives, according to the number he expects to find. The smaller owners club together and fit out a waggon with provisions, so that there may be with one waggon, six or eight men representing as many different brands. The big men, who expect to find perhaps one thousand head, send a waggon of their own with five or six riders. About two days before the time fixed for beginning work, we load a waggon with provisions, according to the number of men who go with it. Each man puts in his own roll of blankets. A driver is provided, who also has to act as cook. Each of the riders is provided with several horses, the usual allowance being about five to a man. A horse herder is generally taken, whose sole duty is to look after the loose horses. When we are ready we make our start, driving the loose horses before us.

On reaching our destination we see waggons dotted about in every spot convenient for camping. The men are for the most part lounging round their campfires, discussing cattle, bragging of the speed of their horses, or describing the various brands of which they are in search.

The next morning we are early astir. The 'boss' of the range we are on, comes along and tells us what he wants us to do. We are to work perhaps two creeks that morning. A party is sent up to the head of each creek to drive the cattle down to the mouth, while a third rounds up the cattle along the river. We bring in any cattle we can find and then our whole party rides down pushing all the cattle before them nearly to the rivers; and wherever we find a convenient level, we round them up. Then the work of cutting out begins. As soon as the cattle have quieted down, the word is given

that one man from each outfit may go in and cut out. One of our party goes in, and whenever he sees an animal bearing one of our brands, he runs it out. When we have got out all our cattle we drive them off towards our waggon. In the meantime two other round-ups have been proceeding, and our 'cuts' from them are brought along and all thrown together, forming the nucleus of what we call our 'day-herd'. . . .

But it is time to get our dinner. When that is over, we tell the cook to take the waggon on up the river about six miles [about 9 km], and there camp. Two of our party are told off to follow with the day-herd, and the rest of us attend a couple more round-ups that take place in the afternoon. . . . The leader of the party divides the night into so many reliefs, and tells each man at what hour he has to go 'on herd'. The next day we work on up the river in the same way, and so on day after day till we have rounded up all the cattle in that section of the country.

Ranch Notes in Kansas, Colorado, Indian Territory and Northern Texas, London, 1884, pp. 84–92, in R. W. Richmond & R. W. Mardock, *A Nation Moving West*, University of Nebraska Press, 1960, pp. 289–90

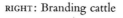
RIGHT: Branding cattle

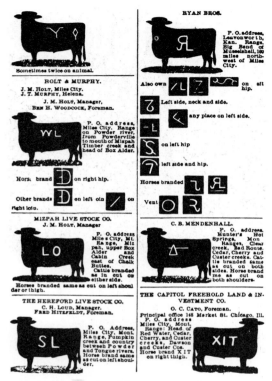

ABOVE: The brands of the X.I.T. ranch

The long drive

SOURCE 74 Managing a trail herd: the recollections of Charles Goodnight

When I made up my mind that I was going to drive, I set about collecting my outfit. My first step toward this was to round up fifty or sixty good horses. Then the mess-waggon was made ready with provisions. Meantime, I informed my neighbour stockmen that I was to drive to a northern market and would receive any cattle they wanted to go with the herd, arranging for the concentration of the herd at some given point, where the cattle were branded with a trail brand. I was never over three days in putting the average herd of three thousand head together.

Our outfits consisted of sixteen to eighteen men, a mess-waggon drawn by four mules, driven by the cook, and a horse wrangler who had charge of the horse herd. These men were thoroughly drilled regarding their places and duties. I always selected two of the most skilled to be my pointers, to handle the front of the herd and keep it on the course given out by the foreman. I always selected three steady men for the rear to look out for the weaker cattle—the drags. The rest of the men were divided along the sides, the swing.

Trail hands were well disciplined and were governed entirely by signals, being too far from the leader to receive orders any other way. The signals were mostly derived from the Plains Indians. They were all made from horseback, by movements of the hat.

The signal to break camp and move upon the trail, simply a motion with the hat in the direction to be followed, was repeated by the pointers and passed along to the rear. About eleven o'clock the signal to graze was passed along the line. Then the men ate dinner, which was prepared while breakfast was cooking. When the cattle began to lie down, the manager knew that they had grazed long enough, and gave the signal to resume the trail.

We always tried to reach water before sun-down. This gave us ample time to have the cattle filled and everything arranged for a pleasant night. The herd was put in a circle, the cattle being a comfortable distance apart. At first, when the cattle were fresh, I used a double guard; that is, half the men guarded the first part of the night, the other half the latter part. In storms or stampedes we were all on duty. After we

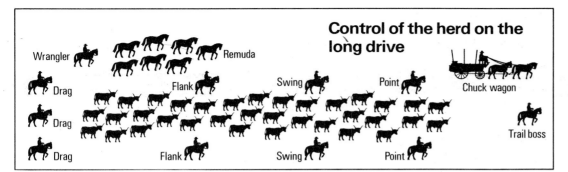

Control of the herd on the long drive

Wrangler · Remuda · Drag · Flank · Swing · Point · Chuck wagon · Trail boss · Drag · Drag · Flank · Swing · Point

had been out a while the men could easily stay awake; in fact, the habit became so firmly fixed that if in camp they would wake at the regular time, and would not be able to sleep during their watch.

J. Evetts Haley, *Charles Goodnight: Cowman and Plainsman*, University of Oklahoma Press, 1949, pp. 245-8

SOURCE 75 'Going up the Texas Trail'; extracts from Jim Herron's description of his first long drive in 1880

Meeting a trail boss

I had always wanted to be a real cowboy. The 'Western Trail', passed close to the range where we held father's cattle. Many big herds passed that way daily in the summer months. One day a herd came swinging into sight. I learned that this herd was heading for the Black Hills in Dakota. I asked what the Boss' name was. They told me 'Quinlan'. When I rode up I asked, 'You need a good man?' The boss stood up high in his stirrups and shaded his eyes with one hand, all the while looking across the prairie. 'Wheah is this man?' he asked. 'I sho don't see Him.' The two men with him howled with laughter. . . .

Warnings

Quinlan warned me against following the cattle trails and leaving home. It was hard work, he told me, just hard work and nothing else. Even growed men nearly died for lack of sleep, he said. He asked if I could ride well. 'Some Injun may lift youh haih, boy,' one of the men remarked. It was true that we would pass through Indian Territory, and the thought of Indians made the fuzz on the back of my neck stand up, but

ABOVE: Cowboys eating outside a chuck wagon by Frederic Remington

ABOVE LEFT: Cowboys directing the herd on the long drive. While the trail boss rode ahead to scout for water and pasture, the cowboys rotated the other duties

I put up a brave front. 'I'm bound to be a cowboy,' I said, 'even if I have to be a bald-headed one without a scalp.'. . .

Heading north

I was assigned eight horses from the remuda, just like the other men had, for we changed two and three times each day. I was the proudest boy in Texas. We headed north the next morning, me riding the drag. This was the worst job with the trail herd because of the thick dust. . . .

A prairie grave

ABOVE: A prairie grave

Everything went well until we reached the Wichita River. That morning Quinlan rode on ahead, as was his practice. We didn't think much of his failure to return until we saw his horse coming back later, dripping wet and lame. Pearl, the straw boss, called the herd off the trail and told us to water them until he found Quinlan. We were at the river crossing for two days while they searched for Quinlan. Then they found Quinlan's body. It was washed up on a sandbar three miles [5 km] down the stream. But we never learned how or why he drowned. We dug a grave on a little knoll a hundred yards south from the river, and there we buried our boss. The lesson I learned from his sad fate was that even a growed man could lose his life on the trail. . . .

Rivers and Indians

Pearl took charge of the outfit now, and we headed on north. We reached Red River. In crossing all rivers it is difficult to get cattle to take to the waters. It was no trouble for them Longhorns to swim the widest rivers, but it was hard to start them. They mostly wanted to drink, then get out, fall back and graze or just stand and beller.

Farther north of Red River a bunch of Indians rode right up to the lead cattle in the herd, turned them off the trail and held up ten fingers to Pearl, asking for ten of those best steers. When we came up alongside I could hear Pearl protesting. 'No, no! Too many. I give you two, no more'! The Indians rode right into the herd like they might cut out what they wanted. I could see Pearl was nervous. 'Squaws and papooses hungry,' a one-eyed brave said to Pearl. 'Git going,' Pearl said. 'Three, no more!'. . .

Dodge City

After a day or two, we moved north again across the Cimarron River. Within a week we were at Dodge. We camped up the river from the town about five miles [8 km] as there were many herds already laying up there near the crossing and the grass was grazed down short. At Dodge we stopped a few days to rest the herd and Pearl sent the waggon in for supplies. This gave all the men a few days to 'see the elephant', as they called it. I went into Dodge with Wes. There was all sorts of ways to spend your money there at Dodge and the town was full of wild women. Wes wouldn't let them women fool around with me very long at a time, though he didn't care how much tiger milk I lapped up at the saloons. . . .

Stampedes

In a few days we headed for Ogallalie, Nebraska. I had now been on the trail for over forty days. It was mighty hard work for a boy of fourteen. There had been only nine of us to handle this big herd after Quinlan's death. Each of us stood guard a quarter of the night and rode all day. During a few storms we rode all night too. But we only had two bad runs with the cattle, and soon milled them and got them back on the bedground. But them stampedes were something frightful to see, and any man's knees will rattle, when the big Longhorns start to run. There was nothing to do then but run with them, stay ahead of them if you could, and turn them into a tight mill when you got the chance, circle them until they was wound up as tight as an eight-day clock on Sunday. It took your best night horse to stay with them. Once we rode alongside the leaders for five miles, then gathered cattle over that five mile stretch all the next day. . . .

The end of the trail

North from Dodge all went quiet and nice. Rance Whitcomb, another boy, decided to quit the herd when we reached Ogallalie. I decided to go with him.

I was about a full-fledged cowboy by this time, I thought, for I could set any bronc rope with the top men and I had even learned to tell time by the stars. . . .

H. E. Chrisman, *Fifty years on the Owl Hoot Trail*, from an original manuscript by Jim Herron, Sage Books, Swallow Press Inc., 1969, pp. 3-14

SOURCE 76 'Cowboys of the old West' by Milt Hinkle, a cowboy who had ridden all the famous trails

It was the duty of the cowboys to ride swift and tough horses from twelve to twenty-four hours every day, with rarely a day of rest. They had to guard those cattle at all hours. Hard and bitter work it was. Only the man who has lived the life of those

ABOVE: A stampede

early ranching days can say just how hard and bitter. The vast distances of the country, the loneliness, the days and nights of solitude were hard, but by no means the worst of their difficulties.

As I muse over my past life it occurs to me that possibly more has been written about the American cowboy, more has been said, more moving-pictures made of and about him, than any other character in American history. I am proud to have been one of those early day cowboys. He is the most romantic, most glamourised and most misunderstood figure ever to ride across the pages of our history.

True West Magazine, No. 47, October 1961, Western Publications Inc.

ABOVE: An Abilene dance house

'The Beef Bonanza, or How to get rich on the plains'

The years from 1880-5 were the hey-day of the cowboy and a time of great prosperity for cattlemen like Iliffe and Goodnight. By that time most of the Indians had been moved onto reservations, and hundreds of hectares of their former hunting grounds were thrown open for grazing the cattle. More railways had been built. New refrigerated rail carriages and cold storage units made it possible for the ranchers to get larger quantities of beef quickly and cheaply to cities all over north and eastern America. Prices for beef were high and there were good profits to be made.

News of these profits even reached Europe where in 1881 many businessmen were eagerly reading a new book written by an American journalist named James Brisbin. The book was called *The Beef Bonanza, or How to get rich on the plains*. This book had a remarkable effect.

Many rich young Britons emigrated to America to set up their own ranches. Hundreds more formed themselves into cattle companies and sent out agents with orders to buy up ranches. French counts and German barons also moved out West. A luxurious cattlemen's club was established in Cheyenne, where these people met for drinks and tennis! Work on the range, however, did not change much under these new ranchmen. The cowboys continued to round up and brand the cattle and to drive them to the railheads.

The end of the open range

By 1885, however, the luck of the cattlemen seems to have run out. Many ranchers, eager to make quick profits, had overstocked their ranges with cattle. Despite warnings about the serious result of this, their herds continued to eat up the grass faster than it could grow. A dry year in 1883 had made matters even worse by shrivelling up the remaining grass. In addition to these troubles beef prices

ABOVE: A cowboy in the rain wearing his slicker (raincape)

ABOVE: Cattle in a blizzard

BELOW: Granville Stuart

began to fall because the cattlemen were producing more beef than the consumers were asking for. Then came the final blow, the dreadful winter of 1886-7.

Granville Stuart who had a ranch in Montana at this time later explained what happened:

SOURCE 77 End of cattle range

During the summer of 1885 more than 100 000 cattle were brought into Montana, most of them trailed up from the South ... and by the fall of 1885 the Montana ranges were crowded. There was no way of preventing the overstocking of the ranges as they were free to all and men felt disposed to take big chances for the hope of large returns.

The spring roundup [of 1886] did not start until May 25, because with the continued drought the green grass would not start. ...

Added to the drought was unprecedented heat. The thermometer stood at 100-110°F and then would come hot winds that licked up every drop of moisture and shrivelled the grass.

This year we noticed that the wild animals moved south. The wild geese and ducks started south early. Everything pointed to a severe winter and we made what preparations we could to meet it with as little suffering to the stock and loss to ourselves as possible.

December 5, there was [a] storm, with the thermometer 12°F below and four inches of snow. On the night of January 15, [the thermometer] stood at 46°F below zero, and there were sixteen inches [40 cm] of snow on the level. It was as though the Arctic regions had pushed down and enveloped us. Everything was white. The storm lasted ten days without abating. The cattle drifted before the storm and fat young steers froze to death along their trails.

There was a series of storms in February and while not so severe yet they came at a time when the cattle were least able to withstand them and there were heavy losses then.

The herds that were driven up from the south and placed on the range late in the summer, perished outright. Others lost from 75-80 [per cent] of their cattle.

It was impossible to tell just what the losses were for a long time as the cattle drifted so badly in the big January storm. We did not get some of ours back for a year. Our entire losses for the year were 66 [per cent] of the herd. In the fall of 1886 there were more than one million head of cattle on the Montana ranges and the losses in the 'big storm' amounted to twenty million dollars. This was the death knell to the range cattle business on anything like the scale it had been run on before.

Charles Russell, 'The Cow Boy Artist', told the story of the 'snuffing out of the big ranges' most graphically in his charcoal sketch, *The Last of 5000*. Charlie was in charge of a herd in the Judith Basin, when the owner, who lived in Helena, wrote and asked how his cattle were getting along? For answer Charlie sent him the sketch.

The large outfits were the heaviest losers as they could not feed or shelter their immense herds. The rancher with a good body of hay land and from 100-200 head of cattle was the man that profited. He had hay enough to feed through storms and could gather his cattle around the ranch and partially shelter them, and in the spring he was enabled to buy cattle cheap.

Granville Stuart, *Forty Years on the Frontier*, pp. 231-7

RIGHT: *Waiting for a chinook or the last of 5000* by Charles Russell, 1887

The fencing of the range

The winter of 1886-7 marked the beginning of the end of cattle ranching as most cowboys and cattlemen had known it. Many ranchers began to realise that in future they would have to keep the grass and the cattle in balance. This could not be done on the open range if their neighbours continued to increase their herds and to allow their cattle to overgraze the grass. The only solution was to fence the land, and use some of it for growing hay for winter fodder. The herds would have to be cut in size and then moved from pasture to pasture to allow the grass to grow again.

Barbed wire and windmills

Two technical inventions played a most important part in bringing about these changes in cattle ranching. One of them was the discovery of a cheap, effective way of fencing land. This was barbed wire, patented in 1874 by Joseph Glidden. The second, a mechanical device, the portable windpump (or windmill) enabled the rancher to fence off his land even where there was no water. With the aid of the windpump he could then draw water up from underground. The final impetus was given by the cattlemen's rivals, the farmers who were also moving onto the High Plains and fencing off their 160 acre [64 hectare] plots all over the range. So ranchers, too, were finally forced to fence their land.

If the end of the open range brought new ways of ranching for the cattlemen, it also brought great changes in the life of the cowboy. The fences and pasturing of cattle brought an end to the round up and the long drive. Some cowboys looked back with regret to the days when they were riding the open range and roping cattle instead of mending fences and windmills. The hey-day of the cowboy lasted only thirty years, from 1860-90. By the middle of the twentieth century they were no longer only riding horses but using jeeps, pick-up trucks and even helicopters.

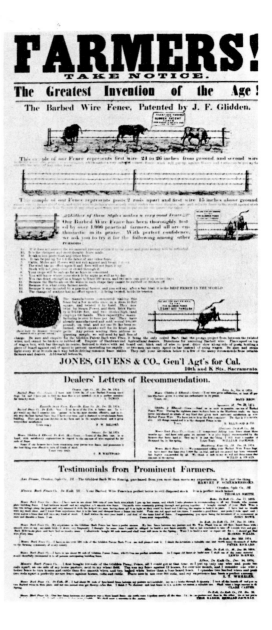

RIGHT: The first poster to advertise barbed wire, 1874
ABOVE: Riding the fence and the mill

4
The homesteaders

As the cattlemen were gradually moving onto the High Plains from the south and then the west, the farmers (or homesteaders as they are often called) began moving onto the prairies from the east. The homesteaders are important in the history of the American West because their attitude to the Great Plains was different from that of the other people who made their homes there. They did not come prepared to adapt themselves to the land and its environment as the Indians and cattlemen had done. The homesteaders wanted to change it to fit a new way of life—that of the cultivator and tiller of the soil. The history of the homesteaders is like a play with three acts. In the first act, we see the homesteaders facing great difficulties when they tried to farm on the plains using the methods and crops they brought with them from the East. In the second act, we see how the farmers were eventually forced to adapt themselves to the environment of the plains. They were forced to develop new farming methods which took account of the difficulties caused by the soil and climate of the plains. In the last act, we see how, with the aid of these new methods and, also new mechanical and technical inventions, the farmers finally became the first people to tame this land. They were the first white men and women to build up a new way of life on the plains.

The homesteaders move West

In the 1850s the soil and climate of the Great Plains were not, as we have seen, the only obstacles to the settlement of this area. The land west of Missouri, Arkansas and Iowa was still officially set aside as Indian territory, and therefore not

OPPOSITE: Peter M. Barnes and his family in front of their sod dug-out in Custer county, Nebraska, 1887

Proposed survey of the first seven ranges under the Ordinance of 1785

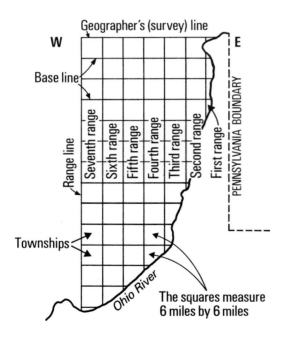

The squares measure 6 miles by 6 miles

open for settlement by white men. In 1854, however, after treaties of sale with Indians, the territories of Kansas and Nebraska were created and opened to the white men (see Fig. 2). Between 1854 and 1865 the first farmers began to settle in the prairie grasslands on the eastern edge of the Great Plains. Except for a shortage of trees, this area was not very different from their homelands east of the Mississippi. It had gently rolling hills, rich brown soil and a fairly dependable rainfall. As a result farmers were able to grow their familiar crops of maize and vegetables. It was only in the years following the Civil War (1861-5) that settlers began to move out to the drier lands of the central and western parts of the Great Plains. Between 1870 and 1900 more land was settled and placed under cultivation than in all the previous history of the American continent. By 1890 farms and cattle ranches were scattered in all regions of the Great Plains. Only the worst desert and mountain regions had failed to attract some settlers.

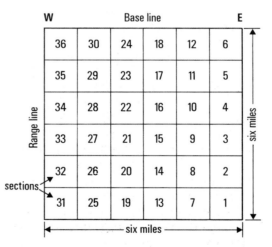

A township as numbered under the Ordinance of 1785

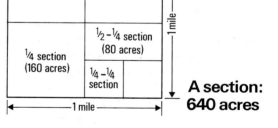

A section: 640 acres

Fig. 2. You may have noticed when looking at maps of North America that the boundaries of American States are very straight compared with boundaries of European countries or English counties. This is because from the 1780s onwards, the American federal government devised a systematic plan for the settlement of new land. All new land in the West opened for settlement became *public domain*, owned initially by the federal government. Before it was *officially* opened for settlement and sold (or granted) to newcomers, government land had first to be surveyed in a series of ranges. (This, of course, did not prevent settlers from moving in before the survey, though they had no legal claim to the land.) This land was then divided into areas called townships, 6 miles square. Some townships could be sold as a whole. Others were further divided into *sections* of 1 mile square (640 acres). In each township Congress reserved four sections for later disposal, and set one section aside to maintain common schools. The rest were sold by auction at a minimum price: at first, this was 1 dollar an acre. Many ordinary families could not afford to pay 640 dollars to buy a section. As a result, sometimes whole townships were bought by land speculators at these auctions. The diagrams on p. 88 show the ranges, a township and a section.

Why go West?

Who then were these settlers? Where did they come from? Why, after 1865, did so many people wish to move into a land which most Americans had previously thought unsuitable for agriculture?

The lure of the land

There were, in fact, many different kinds of people who wished to move out onto the plains. As a result, they had a wide variety of motives. In general, however, the new settlers fell into three main groups.

There were former Negro slaves who wanted to leave their plantation homes in the South after the Civil War (1861-5). Many of them were driven West either by the persecution which followed the withdrawal of federal troops from the South, or by economic problems affecting the plantations. During the 'Exodus' of 1879 between 20 000 and 40 000 Negroes set off for Kansas, some walking up the Chisholm trail, others travelling by boat up the Mississippi.

Then there were the immigrants from Europe. Most of these made their way over the Great Lakes into the prairie lands of Iowa and Minnesota. Scandinavians came in search of good farming land. Mennonites came from Europe in search of political and religious freedom. Many English, Irish, Scottish and German families emigrated to America to escape from poverty and unemployment.

Finally there was the third and by far the largest group of settlers: white Americans from east of the Mississippi— farmers, tradesmen, lawyers and politicians and many others. Some of the men had political ambitions and were anxious to obtain posts in the governments of the newly formed territories. There, judges, peace officers, surveyors, tax collectors and many other officials were all needed.

TOP: Emigrants moving to Custer county, Nebraska, 1886

ABOVE: Former slaves, 'very highly respected citizens', mark their new lives as landowners by posing outside their sod house for a photograph

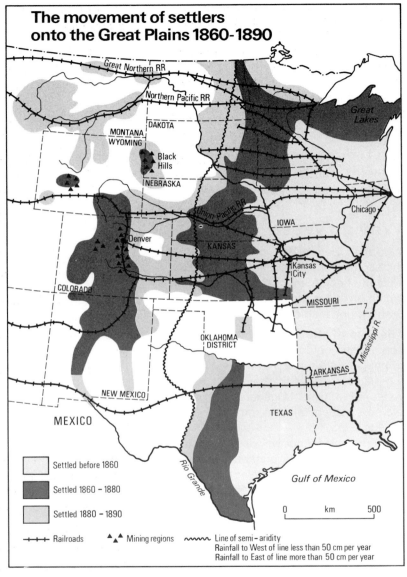

The movement of settlers onto the Great Plains 1860-1890

Great Northern RR
Northern Pacific RR
DAKOTA
MONTANA
WYOMING
Black Hills
NEBRASKA
Union Pacific RR
Denver
IOWA
Chicago
KANSAS
Kansas City
COLORADO
MISSOURI
Mississippi R.
OKLAHOMA DISTRICT
ARKANSAS
NEW MEXICO
TEXAS
MEXICO
Rio Grande
Gulf of Mexico
Great Lakes

Settled before 1860

Settled 1860 – 1880

Settled 1880 – 1890

0   km   500

╫╫ Railroads   ▲▲ Mining regions   ∿∿ Line of semi-aridity
Rainfall to West of line less than 50 cm per year
Rainfall to East of line more than 50 cm per year

Land speculators and town promoters were also often at the head of the race into new territories. These men made their living by buying up vast areas of newly surveyed government land at a low price and then selling it later at a higher price to settlers (source 78). Besides these men, many ordinary families moved West after 1860. Most of these had practical and down to earth motives for wanting to leave their homes (sources 79, 80). The most important of these reasons, however, was the desire for new farming land.

SOURCE 78 The city of New Babylon as it was advertised on paper and as it really was

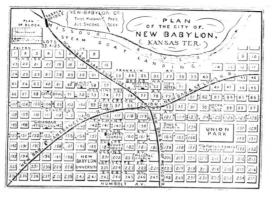

Albert D. Richardson, *Beyond the Mississippi*, American Publishing Co., 1867

SOURCE 79 The soldiers go West

The great prairies beckoned the mustered out soldiers of the Civil War. They had learned the spirit of adventure in the armies of Tennessee and Virginia. The home nest was now too small for them. Soon they were swarming to Nebraska and Kansas where free homes waited them, where the soil was fertile and the climate congenial.

Dr Cass G. Barns, *The Sod House*, University of Nebraska Press, Bison Books, 1970, p. 255

SOURCE 80 A doctor goes West: a personal memory by Dr Cass G. Barns

In 1878 I was a young doctor in the beautiful town of Laporte, Indiana. I had noted with great interest the passage of 'prairie schooners' westward bound. Their objective was Kansas or Nebraska where they hoped to establish themselves in homes of their own instead of renting farms in the older states owned by landlords. Many waggons had mottoes painted on the white waggon covers: 'Kansas or Bust' and Horace Greeley's advice, 'Go West, young man'.

Then Nebraska railroads began to advertise for settlers and offer wonderful inducements to buy their lands and settle on them. Great effort was made to entice 'settlers'. Among the propositions was the Pawnees' reservation land in Nebraska that had just been surveyed and offered for sale at very low prices. During November 1878, I determined to see Nebraska for myself, and if the land looked good, to secure some of it while it was cheap.

Barns, *The Sod House*, pp. 31, 32, 36, 37

A HABITABLE DWELLING

A HOUSE "TWELVE BY FOURTEEN"

A BONA FIDE RESIDENCE

The Homestead Act 1862

Many white settlers who headed for the plains came from the Mississippi valley. Here population had been increasing steadily and many pioneering farmers felt their area was becoming too crowded and decided to move on yet again (source 81). These farmers, and would-be farmers, were drawn further West by the offer of free land. Before 1862 the settlers were allowed to claim 160 acres (64 hectares) of public land for the minimum current price of $1.25 an acre. But even this small sum was too much for many would-be farmers. For many years they had been demanding the right to free land. Finally in 1862 the Homestead Act was passed. This allowed settlers to claim 160 acres of free land if they lived and worked on it for five years. The thought of free land attracted large numbers of settlers though many were to be disappointed. Much of the best land had been given either to the railroads or to the governments of the new territories to build and finance schools and other public buildings. Forty per cent of the land in Kansas was given away and so made unavailable to homesteaders. Moreover, there were loop-holes in the Act which allowed much of the remaining land to be dishonestly claimed by land-grabbers. In the end many farmers had little choice but to buy land or settle on poorer homestead claims. This was to add to their problems, as we shall see later.

SOURCE 81 The move to the wilderness of Kansas, 1855, described by Thomas Allen Banning

When I was several years old my father sold his farm in Illinois and moved his family to the wilds of Kansas. The older boys were growing to be big husky lads. Kansas had just been thrown open for people to enter and take up farms; Indians, hunters and trappers were about the only people there. But in the early fifties, men who wanted Kansas to be a slave state and men who wanted it to be free began to move in. So as my father wanted Kansas to become a free state, he went there to help and vote to bring it about.

Then, too, my father thought that Illinois was getting pretty well settled up. You often see three or four farm houses from a single hill top. And so my father, like others, grew restless and wanted to move West to where the great prairies rolled away, mile after mile. But the deciding motive that caused my father to tear things up by the roots, was the lure of land that could be had practically without money by those who would settle on it, and convert it into farms. Land was a mighty motive to a man who had sons growing to manhood. He wanted them to have the opportunity of taking adjoining lands and settling on farms around him. And so he decided to go.

Paul M. Angle (ed.), *Narratives of Noah Harris Letts and Thomas Allen Banning 1825-1865*, R. R. Donnelly & Sons, Lakeside Press, 1972, pp. 157, 161

Glowing newspaper reports

Whatever their reason for wanting to leave their homes, native Americans and foreign immigrants were also lured towards the Great Plains by glowing newspaper reports about the golden opportunities in the West. These advertisements and articles were placed in the newspapers by a number of different people (source 82).

First there were the governments of the new territories. They were obviously keen to sell the land lots in the new townships and set up farms and industries. As soon as the population of a territory reached 60 000 it could apply to be admitted to the Union as a full state. Once a territory became a state there would be more important jobs in the state government. Immigration boards were set up to encourage settlers. They placed advertisements in newspapers all over America and Europe describing the delights of the new territories.

This publicity drew thousands of settlers from Europe where immigration bureaux were also set up with agents hired to spread propaganda. Some foreign immigrants in their turn wrote home and urged their fellow countrymen and women to follow them (source 83).

OPPOSITE: Dishonest land claims: settlers could stake claim to land if they built a house at least 12 by 14— unfortunately the regulations failed to specify feet or inches!
BELOW: Gathering pumpkins and husking maize

SOURCE 82 The wonders of Kansas agriculture as reported in the 'Coolidge Border Ruffian' 10 July 1886

There is no doubt . . . that Missouri is a great country, but it will not compare for a moment with Kansas. Think of the Kansas pumpkins! Gentlemen, when I was on a farm in that glorious country I once lost three cows. For three weeks I searched in vain and was returning home when I suddenly heard the tinkle of a cowbell. Investigation showed that the cows were inside a pumpkin, eating calmly. How did they get in, you say? Well, the pumpkin vines grew rapidly there, and dragged a pumpkin over the rough ground until a hole was worn in the side, through which the cows entered. I afterwards had it cured and used it for a waggon shed.

Is it a good country for corn, you ask? Stranger, you'll never know what a corn country is until you go to Kansas. When the husking is done in the fall the men go out with mallets and wedges and split up the corn-stalks for shipment to the East as telegraph poles. Four horses are then hitched to each ear.

Richmond and Mardock, *A Nation moving West*, p. 314

SOURCE 83 Extracts from a letter published in a Norwegian newspaper in August 1869

Minnesota, July 1869

It is not only my opinion but that of all who have seen it that this land presents so many advantages for Scandinavian farmers that immigrants are likely to stream in here within the next year. The soil is fertile and there is not as much as a stone or a stump in the way of the plow. Railroads are to run through the middle of the valley. In the summer months, May, June, July and August, the heat may at times be great, but the atmosphere is always fresh. In the wintertime, the snow is usually two or three feet deep and lies in a solid mass over the whole prairie.

Paul Hjelm Hansen

Theodore C. Blegen (ed.), *Land of their choice: the immigrants write home*, University of Minnesota Press, 1955, p. 441

ABOVE: Swedish immigrants to Kansas

The railroads

It was the railway companies, however, who played the greatest part in attracting settlers to the West. Plans for a railway line across North America to the west coast began to be discussed around 1860. The federal government in Washington was very keen to have a rail link with Oregon and California. Once a railway line was built, California and Oregon would no longer be so cut off from the eastern states. Easy communications between the west coast and the eastern states would help to prevent any plans for independent republics in California and Oregon. The federal government did not have enough ready money to help the railway companies cover the cost of such a huge scheme. But they did have land— millions of hectares of it in the West. In 1862, therefore, when the federal government gave the Union Pacific and the Central Pacific Railroad Companies permission to build the first railroad across the plains, they also gave them alternate townships on either side of the track. The railroad companies could then sell this land to settlers. In this way they could raise money to pay for the construction of the railroad.

Not only were the railroad companies keen to sell the actual land. They were also eager to attract passengers and freight traffic so that the railway would be profitable once it was built. Passengers and freight traffic would grow only if towns, farms and industries were set up along the side of the railroad track across the plains. The railroad companies, therefore, organised a massive publicity campaign to draw settlers west (source 84). They also provided more practical attractions for would-be immigrants. First, they offered a safe, cheap and speedy journey to the West. Secondly, they even built special 'homes' or 'hotels' at various stopping places along the route. These offered temporary accommodation for families until they found a suitable place for a home of their own. When we think about the long and dangerous journeys faced by the early travellers in their covered wagons, we can easily understand just how important the railways were in attracting settlers to the Great Plains.

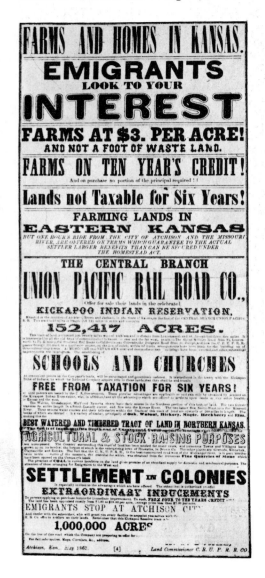

ABOVE: Travelling on an emigrant train

Claiming a homestead and building a home

After the long journey onto the plains, the settlers first had to stake a claim to their land and register their claim at the land office. Next, homesteaders had to build a shelter for themselves and their families. Some settlers in eastern Kansas and Nebraska and also Minnesota (where timber grew along the streams) were able to build log cabins (source 85). By the 1870s, however, settlers began to move out onto the treeless grasslands. They had to make use of the only building material available : sods of prairie grass. Some settlers made themselves dug-outs. These were merely holes cut into a hillside with a front wall of sods. Other homesteaders built sod houses (source 86). Sod houses had their advantages as homes, in that they could not be burned down by prairie fires. But they also had many disadvantages, as the homesteaders soon discovered (sources 87, 88).

SOURCE 85 'The commencement of a home': Thomas Allen Banning's description of the building of his family's first log home in Kansas in 1855

My father and big brothers put up the log house and built a little kitchen in the rear. They were in a great hurry and so the house was a rough affair. The floor was of broad flat pieces split from logs. The chimney was built from broken pieces of rock laid in a sort of clay mortar, with a large flat stone for the fireplace and hearth. The roof was of split out pieces of log. They made a roof, but not very tight or waterproof in case of rain or snow. Openings were made for windows and doors. While the house was being built we lived out of doors, and my mother did her cooking over an open fire.

Angle, *Narratives of Letts and Banning, 1825–1865*, pp. 166–8

SOURCE 86 The cost of building a dug-out: the accounts of Howard Ruede, a homesteader who went to Kansas in 1877

April 10, 1877: I made out an estimate of the cost of our house. This does not include what was paid for in work.

Ridgepole and hauling (including 2 loads of firewood)	$1.50
Rafters and straw	50c
2 lb. nails	50c
Hinges	20c
Window	75c
Total cash paid	$4.05

Then there was $4 of lumber which was paid for in work, and $1.50 for hauling it over, which together with hauling the firewood 50c. makes $10.05 for a place to live in and firewood enough for the summer.

Ruede, *Sod House Days*, p. 43

ABOVE: The first season: homesteaders building a log cabin

SOURCE 87 The arrival of Dr Cass G. Barns and his wife at their new home in Nebraska in 1878

We reached our farm at noon and found the family only waiting our arrival to move to a homestead they had taken for themselves. My wife became unhappy for the first time when she saw bed bugs racing up the walls. My wife had a good thick white-wash made and plastered on the walls and got rid of the bugs.

I set about building a new frame house at once. We had a good sod house by early June but the joints between the layer of sods on the roof required a renewal of fine clay occasionally to keep rain water from trickling through. We laid a board floor in the end of the room back from the stove and by hanging a curtain in the middle had two sleeping rooms where privacy could be observed. When it rained, the roof leaked the dirty water onto our bed and I would wake up with water running through my hair.

Barns, *The Sod House*, pp. 38-40

SOURCE 88 A doctor's views of some advantages and disadvantages of the sod house, by Dr Cass G. Barns

It was not wholly the fault of the sod house that contagious diseases were common. The common drinking cup, the open dug well, the outdoor toilet (or no toilet at all) shared the blame with the lack of ventilation and crowded quarters of the sod house.

The floor of a dugout, or sod house, was commonly of clay dirt. It was not possible to scrub or disinfect it of the millions of germs that found a breeding place in the dirt trodden underfoot. The 'no spitting' fad had not taken root. Disease germs were here, there, everywhere and anywhere. No wonder the mortality by diphtheria was so great among children.

While those houses, as a rule, were warm in winter and fairly cool in summer for the human occupants, they favoured fleas and bed bugs by the million. Added to the lowering of vitality by lack of a balanced ration of food, lack of clothing, and changes of temperature, the wonder is not so much that disease and infection took a heavy toll, as the wonder that so many survived to spend their later lives in modern homes.

Barns, *The Sod House*, pp. 244-7

ABOVE: A mourning Nebraska family visit the grave of their boy who died in 1881, aged 19 months

ABOVE RIGHT: Gathering cow chips (dung) for fuel

A woman's work

The building of the sod house was the homesteaders' first warning that life on the plains would not be same as 'back East'. Nevertheless, they were forced to learn to live in their 'soddy' homes because they had no other choice. The women soon realised that they would have to make changes to their usual methods of cooking, washing and running their homes (source 89). Many household goods such as soap, coffee and sugar were scarce and so substitutes had to be devised. Wood and coal for firing the stove were also un-available and so other fuels had to be found (sources 90, 91). For some women, life was not only hard, it was also lonely (source 92). In other areas, however, settlers lived closer together. Neighbours visited each other. Churches and schools were soon built—also out of prairie sods (source 93).

ABOVE: Homesteaders pose for a photograph with their prize possession

SOURCE 89 The domestic problems of Howard Ruede in his first year on his Kansas homestead in 1877-8

Sunday April 22, 1877 Our household goods, now include 2 buckets, 1 crock, 1 earthen dish, saucepan, 1 spider, 1 tin dish, 3 china plates, 3 pair knives and forks, 3 pie plates, 3 spoons, 3 cups and saucers, 1 cracked china cup for salt and a tin cup. How's that for an outfit?

Sunday May 13, 1877 I gave up wearing socks about 4 weeks ago as there is no water to wash dirty things up at the claim and we could not afford to pay for having them washed.

Ruede, *Sod House Days*, pp. 55, 72

SOURCE 90 'My Mother': described by Thomas Allen Banning

I have often wondered how my mother stood it with such a family of children and no one to help her but my oldest sister. We used candles, which my mother made by pouring melted tallow into moulds. We used soft soap that my mother made by leaching water slowly through a barrel of wood ash to get the alkali and potash, and then boiling this in a kettle with the scraps of fats she saved. Often she would sit up late at night darning our socks and mending our ragged pants. Fortunately for her we ran barefoot from early spring till winter snows. The socks that grew on our feet needed no darning. Occasionally, a travelling shoe-maker would come along and stop a day or two to mend our shoes. Now and then a tinsmith or tinker would come along and solder our pans and kettles.

Angle, *Narratives of Letts and Banning 1825-1865*, pp. 182-3

SOURCE 91 The life of the O'Kieffe family in Nebraska in the 1880s

Naturally the first event in my life was being born which occurred on July 5 1879. According to what I've been told Mother herded cattle all day long in the broiling sun. The next morning around 2 a.m. I was born. No doctor, no nurse, no midwife, just Mother and God; and 2 days later she was up and doing her regular housework.

On our Sheridan County farm, we certainly did find the good earth the only source of things to keep soul and body together. From our fields we gathered corn, wheat, oats and rye. The corn went for cattle feed. We sold our wheat, but now and then

Mother would parch a batch to mix with coffee beans to make [them] last longer. As in most countries, weeds grew in profusion, creating lots of problems. But in the O'Kieffe home, our slogan was: 'If you can't beat 'em, eat 'em'.

For the edification of housewives who may never have cooked with buffalo chips [dung] here is a rundown of the operations that Mother went through when making biscuits. It goes like this: stoke the stove, get out the flour sack, stoke the stove, wash your hands, mix the biscuit dough, stoke the stove, wash your hands, cut out the biscuits with the top of a baking-powder can, stoke the stove, wash your hands, put the pan of biscuits in the oven, keep on stoking the stove until the biscuits are done. Mother had to go through this tedious routine three times a day.

During two or three of our years on the Sheridan County farm, we raised a pretty fair patch of sorghum cane. Old Man Hardy had set up a sorghum mill on his farm and there we hauled our cane stalks. The mill was a simple affair much like a clothes wringer. The cane juice thus crushed out dropped down into a receptacle which was emptied into the nearby cooking tank. Then the fully cooked molasses was drained off ready to be taken home. At home the molasses sure went well on breakfast pancakes, and we also mixed it with lard to make a spread for Mother's homemade bread.

Western Story: the recollections of Charlie O'Kieffe, 1884-1896, University of Nebraska Press, 1960, pp. 3, 26, 36-7, 40

LEFT: A sod dug-out, Nebraska, 1892

SOURCE 92 The isolation of life on prairie farms

In the summer there is a school for the children, one, two or three miles away, but in the winter the distances across the snow covered plains are too great for them to travel in severe weather; the schoolhouse is closed, and there is nothing for them to do but to house themselves and long for spring. Life, shut up in the little wooden farmhouses cannot well be very cheerful. A drive to the nearest town is almost the only diversion. There the farmers and their wives gather in the stores and manage to enjoy a little sociability. The women wish the crop had been better, so that they could buy some of the things of which they are badly in need. The men smoke corncob pipes and talk politics.

There are few social events in the life of these prairie farmers to enliven the monotony of the long winter evenings; no singing schools, spelling schools, debating clubs, or church gatherings. Neighbourly calls are infrequent because of the long distances which separate the farmhouses.

Atlantic Monthly, LXXII, 1893, pp. 378-383

SOURCE 93 Community life in a Nebraska neighbourhood in 1878

Our neighbourhood people were a fine class of people. Social gatherings were common and the lunches of fried chicken, cake and delicacies. The sod school house had given way to a small frame building just before we arrived. The school district was the fourth one organised in the county. I was made a member of the school board and at once began to agitate for the employing of a higher qualified teacher, and a nine month school term was held. It proved so satisfactory that the patrons approved a still longer term and decided to build the school house larger. This house became the public hall for all entertainments, social gatherings, Sunday School and religious services.

Barns, *The Sod House*, pp. 42-3

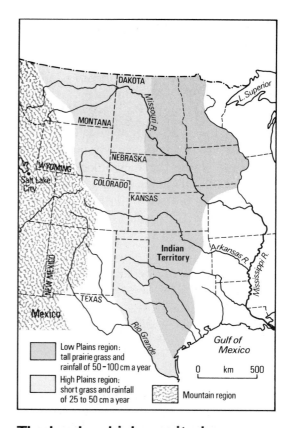

The lands which awaited the farmers when they moved onto the Great Plains

The problems of the farmer

Though the women were soon forced to adapt to a new life on the plains, most of the farmers were not so quick to change their old ways. In the 1860s little was known in detail about the rainfall pattern of the plains except that it appeared to be scanty. Even less was known about the kind of crops and methods necessary for successful farming in this area.

Government reports and travellers' descriptions were full of warnings to prospective homesteaders about farming in the plains. But farmers either did not read them or took little notice. Most farmers moved West convinced that they could farm their land using the same crops and methods as in the rich well watered land of the East. The problems they faced, however, eventually made them think again.

Ploughing, harvesting and threshing

First the farmers had to plough, or 'break' the thick prairie sod. This was a slow and back-breaking job which earned them the nickname of 'sodbusters'. Many young farmers did not bring a suitable plough or could not afford to buy one immediately. They often paid a neighbour to break the sod for them while they earned some cash to buy food and equipment.

In addition to their lack of money, many farmers were short of men to help them on the farm. Until the 1860s, harvesting and threshing had to be done by hand (source 94), but on the plains there were no casual labourers to help with the harvest. As early as 1831, Cyrus McCormick had invented a mechanical harvester but this had been of little use in the hilly wooded lands of the East. Therefore, few people had bought it. It was very expensive to buy—too expensive for poor farmers on the Great Plains.

ABOVE: Breaking the soil on a Kansas prairie farm, 1868

SOURCE 94 Our wheat-cutting and threshing, recalled by Thomas Allen Banning

My father also took seed when we moved to Kansas. It was what is known as winter wheat. That fall my father sowed [two hectares] of wheat. He would carry a peck or so in a bag hung around his neck and shoulder, and with his right hand would take out a handful and fling it out from side to side over the ground as evenly as he could. This was called broadcasting it.

When the wheat got ripe the next summer, he cut or harvested it with a cradle [a kind of scythe]. Some one would then gather up the little piles and bind them by hand into bundles and set a dozen or so together in a shock. This is the way we harvested our wheat. There were no big reaping and binding machines drawn by horses or motor to cut and bind the grain as the farmers have now.

And there were no threshing machines like they have now. In those days, when the shocks were dry enough the farmers would haul them in and spread them on a platform of boards in a circle and shell out the grains by driving horses or oxen round and round the circle to trample out the grains. Another way they used was for men and boys to beat out the grain with flails. A flail was a long handle with a club tied to its end with a stout piece of cord or a buckskin thong.

After the wheat was threshed it was full of chaff and dust and broken pieces of straw. To clean the wheat, my father had to winnow it. He would wait for a day when a good wind was blowing, and then he would spread a sheet on the ground and take the wheat and chaff in a bucket, stand on a chair and pour out a thin stream onto the sheet. The wind would blow the light chaff and trash away and the heavy grain would fall in a heap. He then took this to a little grist mill a few miles away and had it ground into flour, which your great grandmother made into bread, and which your grandfather ate. There were no bakeries or shops where we could go and buy loaves of bread as your mothers can.

Angle, *Narratives of Letts and Banning, 1825-65*, pp. 187-90

TOP: Harvesting with a grain cradle (scythe)
ABOVE: Threshing with flails

ABOVE: Winnowing

Fencing

The lack of timber for fencing also proved a great problem. Most farmers could not afford to buy timber from the East. Hedging plants were also expensive. This made it difficult for farmers to keep cattle off their crops, and caused trouble between farmers and cattlemen, as we shall see later.

Lack of water

The lack of water was a much more serious problem, except in eastern Kansas and Nebraska. Out on the High Plains the average rainfall was only 38 cm a year—not sufficient for normal agriculture. But to make matters worse, most of this rain fell between April and November when the sun and hot summer winds quickly evaporated all moisture from the soil. During the growing season 75-100 cm of water were actually lost in this way on the plains.

Since the crops could not be watered by rain, other ways had to be found. Few farmers except those near the Rockies had streams on their land and so irrigation was not possible. In any case irrigation schemes would have demanded cooperative effort and capital. Some farmers tried to dig open wells from which, as in the East, they could raise water with a bucket. But on the plains this was no simple matter. Digging the heavy prairie soil was difficult enough anyway but the water table was so low that in places shafts of 150 m were necessary. Even then a strike was not a certainty for it was difficult to locate underground water with only a divining rod. But water had to be found and thousands of farmers did dig their wells. Even if they were successful this was not a complete answer.

A well could hold enough water for a family and their animals but it could not keep 160 acres (64 hectares) of crops irrigated throughout the summer. Furthermore, in 1865, neither the farmers nor the federal government realised that in regions with only 25-40 cm of rainfall a year, a 160 acre farm was not big enough to support a man and his family. Because of the lack of water, the crop yields were too low.

Droughts and grasshoppers

In normal years farmers found it difficult enough to make a living on the plains. Then in the 1860s they suffered a series of terrible droughts. Between January 1859 and November 1860 no rain fell in Nebraska and Kansas. The earth cracked open and crops shrivelled up (source 95). Then came summer hailstorms and prairie fires which devastated south west Minnesota in the summer of 1871. The final blow came from the plague of grasshoppers which swarmed through the prairies in the 1870s, devouring everything in their path (source 96). Most families had no money to buy either more seeds or even food. For winter after winter in the early 1870s thousands of people went hungry. The governments of Kansas,

Nebraska and Minnesota were forced to raise relief funds to prevent these homesteaders from starving or returning to the East in their thousands. The disasters of the 1870s brought an end to the illusions of many families about life on the Great Plains (sources 97-99).

LEFT: Fighting a prairie fire, 1874

SOURCE 95 'Drouthy Kansas', a painting by Henry Worrall

RIGHT: *Drouthy Kansas*, a painting by Henry Worrall. This painting was designed to contradict the bad publicity about the droughts which were deterring settlers from moving to Kansas

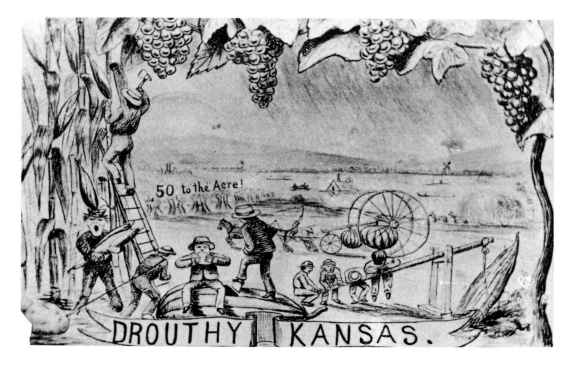

SOURCE 96 The grasshopper plague of 1874

We were at the table; the usual midday meal was being served; one of the youngsters who had gone to the well to fill the water pitcher came hurrying in. 'They're here! The sky is full of 'm. The whole yard is crawling with the nasty things'. Food halfway to the mouth fell back upon the plate. Without speaking the whole family passed outside. Sharp spats in the face, insects alighted on the shoulders, in the hair, scratchy rustlings on the roofs, disgusted brushing of men's beards, the frightened whimper of a child. 'Are they going to eat us up?' Over head, the sun, dimmed like the beginning of an eclipse, glinted on silvery wings as far as eyes could pierce; leaves of shade trees, blades of grass and weedstems bending with the weight on clinging inch-long horrors.

Not much was said. Men and boys got out the corn-knives and set out for the corn-fields. Before sunset they came back, weary and dispirited, the cornstalks, they said, were already naked as beanpoles. The garden truck had disappeared, even the dry onions were gone, leaving smooth moulds in the ground empty as uncorked bottles. Fruit hung on the leafless branches, gnawed to the core. The woods looked thin as in late autumn.

Water troughs and loosely covered wells were foul with drowned 'hoppers. A young wife awaiting her first baby, in the absence of her husband had gone insane from fright, 'all alone in that sun-baked shanty on the bald prairie'. Eggs and milk tasted of the 'hoppers.

William John Meredith, 'The Old Plum Grove Colony in Jefferson County', *Kansas Historical Quarterly*, VII, November 1938, pp. 364-5, Kansas State Historical Society

SOURCE 97 Extract from a letter written by Jennie Flint of Minnesota to Governor Davis, applying for assistance for herself and her 71 year old father, 6 February 1874

We have no money nor nothing to sell to get any more clothes with as the grass-hoppers destroyed all of our crops (what few we had—for we have not much land broke as yet as we have no team of our own we have to hire one). We managed to raise a few potatoes and some corn and a little buckwheat and that is all we have to depend on. We are very bad off for bedding not having but two quilts and two sheets in the house. We have to use our clothing that we wear on the beds to keep us from

ABOVE: Grasshoppers stopping a westbound train on the Union Pacific Railroad in Nebraska in 1875. Their crushed bodies made the track too slippery

suffering with the cold and then it is most impossible to keep warm for our house is so open. We almost perish here sometimes with the cold. . . . Now if you will be so kind as to send us some bedding and clothes and yarn to knit us some stockings, or send us some money, we would be thankful. . . .

Governor's File No. 320: Minnesota State Archives, in G. C. Fite, *The Farmers' Frontier 1865-1900*, Holt, Rinehart & Winston, pp. 60-1

SOURCE 98 'My Government Claim', a ballad giving one man's view of a homesteader's life on the plains

My name is Tom Hight, an old Bach'lor I am,
You'll find me out West in the county of fame,
You'll find me out West on an elegant plain,
A-starvin' to death on my government claim.

Hurrah for Greer County, the land of the free,
The land of the bedbug, grasshopper and flea,
I'll sing of its praises, I'll tell of its fame,
While starving to death on my government claim.

My House it is built out of national soil,
Its walls are erected according to Hoyle,
Its roof has no pitch, but is level and plain,
I always get wet if it happens to rain.

My clothes are all ragged, my language is rough,
My bread is corndodgers, both solid and tough,
But yet I am happy and live at my ease,
On sorghum molasses and bacon and cheese.

How happy I am when I crawl into bed,
A rattlesnake hisses a tune at my head,
A gay little centipede all without fear,
Crawls over my pillow and into my ear.

Now all you claimholders, I hope you will stay,
And chew your hardtack till you're toothless and grey,
But as for myself I'll no longer remain
To starve like a dog on my government claim.

Farewell to Greer County, farewell to the West,
I'll travel back East to the girl I love best,
I'll travel to Texas and marry me a wife
Cry quits on corndodgers the rest of my life.

Alan Lomax (ed.), *The Penguin Book of American Folk Songs*, Penguin Books, 1964, pp. 109-10

SOURCE 99 'A farmer's life is not a happy one' or 'The woes of Western Agriculture,' a cartoon from 'Puck's Papers', 1887

A new way of farming: 1880-1895

The disasters of the 1870s made the farmers think again. They finally realised that they would not be able to farm in the old way in this new land. Some way had to be found to overcome the problems of shortage of labour, lack of timber and lack of water.

New inventions

New mechanical inventions helped the farmer to solve the first of these problems. Improved mechanical reapers, binders and threshers were in great demand during the Civil War when men were in the army. By 1880 they were cheaper to buy. With their help the farmers could cultivate larger areas of land without needing to employ extra men. Instead they hired a seasonal threshing crew who harvested the wheat on farm after farm.

Barbed wire, patented by Joseph Glidden in 1874, brought a cheap and efficient means of fencing off fields. This simple invention had extremely important results. We had already seen the changes it made to the cattle ranches and the life of the cowboy.

But none of these inventions would be of any use unless the farmer had enough water for his crops. This problem was solved in part by two mechanical aids; the windpump and the well driller which bored the necessary hole. The windpump made use of the constant prairie breezes to raise a continuous supply of water without any effort on the farmer's part. But windpumps were expensive and in any case there was still not enough underground water to irrigate thousands of

BELOW: Windpump outside a Nebraska homestead, 1880s

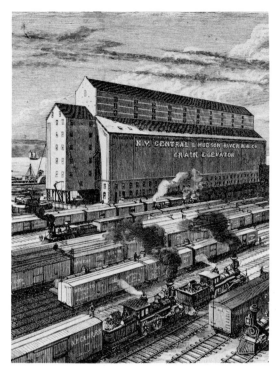

ABOVE: Grain supplies arriving at New York, 1877
LEFT: Steam powered threshing in Dakota in 1879

hectares of crops. It was at this point, when mechanical aids could do no more, that the farmers were forced to change their methods of cultivation.

The Timber and Culture Act

The federal government eventually realised that 160 acres was too small an area for farming in a dry climate. From 1873 onwards they therefore allowed farmers to claim a further 160 acres of free land if they planted one half-acre of trees. The Timber and Culture Act really did help many homesteaders with too little land to make a living.

New methods: dry farming

But it was the introduction of 'dry farming' methods which brought the best solution to the water problems. 'Dry farming' enabled the farmers to grow better crops by making the best use of the moisture already in the ground. In certain years, therefore, farmers had to allow their land to remain fallow so that moisture was not used. They also had to plough their land after every fall of rain or snow and then cover the surface with a fine layer of dust. This ensured that the moisture was ploughed into the soil and then prevented from evaporating.

Dry farming methods also meant that farmers had to grow the kinds of plants which can withstand drought, but still produce good crops. Maize (or corn-on-the-cob), the most familiar crop to American farmers, needed a lot of rain in spring before it would give a good yield.

Soft winter and spring wheats also needed to be grown where there was plenty of rain and no frost. Hard winter wheat, however, such as Turkey Red, proved to be an ideal crop for farmers on the Great Plains. This was brought to America by immigrants from the Crimea in 1874. It could withstand frost and still grow in winter and spring when there was most moisture. The only problem with the hard wheats was that no satisfactory method of milling them had yet been devised. The traditional mill stones splintered the husks into such fine fragments that the flour was left dirty, rancid and so unsaleable. Once again technicians and inventors were called in to solve the farmers' problem. By 1881, a new method of milling hard wheat with rollers was devised. The future of hard wheats and dry farming was assured.

Dry farming methods helped many farmers. By the end of the 1880s they were able to grow enough wheat for their own needs and plenty more to spare. They even began to export wheat by the ship-load to Britain and other European countries.

A new way of life

The problems caused by lack of water were never completely overcome. But by 1890 the farmers and the homesteaders had successfully made a new way of life for themselves: a way of life which was not completely dominated by the environment of the Great Plains.

5
The fate of the Plains Indians

We have seen how in the years between 1860 and 1890 miners and farmers, cowboys and cattlemen gradually moved out to the West and made a new way of life there. But what was the effect of this on the first inhabitants of the plains, the Indians? If you look at the maps and statistics below (pp. 114-5) you will see.

How did this change come about? Why and how did such a fate befall the Indians? The story is a sad one—of bitter fighting and killings, of treachery and broken promises on both sides. It is important, therefore, to try and understand both points of view: that of the Indian and that of the whiteman.

OPPOSITE: Plains Indians with horse-drags

The situation in 1840: A permanent Indian frontier

In 1840 an imaginary line ran north to south along the edge of the Great Plains, west of the Mississippi River. It marked the Permanent Indian Frontier. This was a line beyond which no white man was to be allowed to settle. It was also a line behind which the Indians would be free to hunt and wander in peace for evermore. The line did not exist in the minds of the Plains Indians. The Permanent Indian Frontier was an idea created by the United States government. They hoped that it would solve what they called 'the Indian Problem' once and for all.

The 'Indian Problem' of 1840
In 1840 'the Indian Problem' was not that of the Plains Indians, but of the Eastern Woodland Indians. They were the

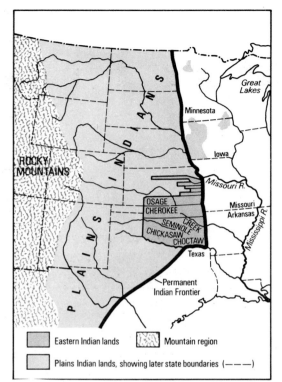

Indian lands on the Great Plains in 1840

Legend:
- Eastern Indian lands
- Mountain region
- Plains Indian lands, showing later state boundaries (———)

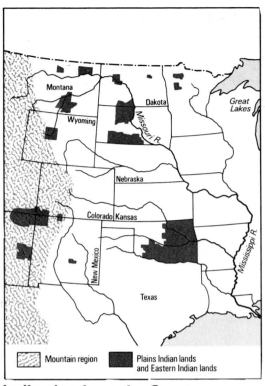

Indian lands on the Great Plains in 1900

Legend:
- Mountain region
- Plains Indian lands and Eastern Indian lands

Fig. 3

	1840	1885
Estimated number of Indians	500 000	270 000
Estimated number of buffalo	13 000 000	200

inhabitants of the eastern coastlands and mountains before the white men came to North America. The white settlers had devised their own methods of dealing with these Indians, tribes like the Creeks, Seminoles, Cherokees and Chocktaws, long before they had even heard about the Plains Indians. Their policy had two conflicting aspects. On one hand they recognised that the Indians had a right to the land since they were the original inhabitants of North America. On the other hand, however, they felt that as the number of white settlers grew, they should have the right to take over this land from the Indians (sources 100, 101).

From the earliest days of white settlement in the sixteenth century, white men had been buying land from the Indians by means of treaties. These were written agreements between Indians and settlers in which the Indians agreed to hand over their lands in exchange for money or goods such as rifles and jewellery. Sometimes the Indians freely agreed to make such treaties. At other times, however, they were cheated or forced into giving away their lands.

The Eastern Indians gradually became the victims of an ever advancing line of white settlers. Some tribes were wiped out by European diseases such as smallpox or measles. Many were badly affected by cheap whisky and spirits. The rest were pushed further and further west.

SOURCE 100 Thomas Jefferson's attitude to the Indian lands in 1786 (he became Secretary of State in 1789)

It may be regarded as certain, that not a foot of land will ever be taken from the Indians, without their own consent. The sacredness of their rights is felt by all thinking persons in America.

J. L. Foley (ed.), *The Jeffersonian Cyclopaedia*, Funk & Wagnall, 1900, p. 122

SOURCE 101 Extract from a letter written by Jefferson to John Adams (US President 1797–1801) in 1812

The Indians [already] backward [in civilisation] will be thrown further back. They will relapse into barbarism and misery and we shall be obliged to drive them with beasts of the forest into the stony [Rocky] mountains.

Foley, *Jeffersonian Cyclopaedia*, pp. 422–3

Plans for 'The Great Removal'

Some tribes like the Cherokee took the 'whiteman's road' and began to learn farming, reading and writing, and even set up their own governments. They hoped that in this way they would be allowed to stay on their lands. But this was not to be. For one thing, many settlers believed that only they could make full use of such land. Indians, they believed, should not be allowed to settle in areas where white men wished to live. In addition to this many white men distrusted and feared the Indians or despised them, like their negro slaves, as an inferior race. Throughout the eighteenth century there were frequent wars during which the Indians fought to prevent the white men from taking their land.

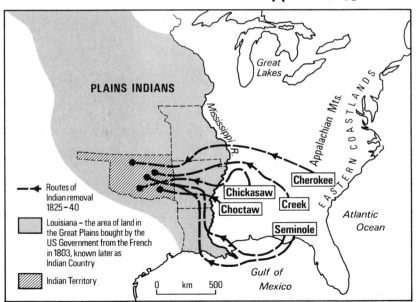

The removal of Eastern Indians to land west of the Mississippi 1825-40

Since the white Americans were not prepared to let the Eastern Indians live amongst them, the only solution was to remove them—but where to? In 1803 the answer came: the American President, Thomas Jefferson bought 'Louisiana' from the French. Louisiana territory was a vast area of land between the Mississippi and the Rocky Mountains. The American government sent explorers to inspect their new territory. We already know what reports they brought back to the government. 'A land wholly unfit for cultivation,' they said, in short, a desert fit only for Indians. Here was the ideal place to send the Eastern Indians.

The 'Trail of Tears'

In 1823 John C. Calhoun, the United States Secretary of War, proposed to President Monroe that all Indians living east of the Mississippi should be moved to lands in the Great American Desert west of the 95th Meridian. In this way all their valuable land could be opened to white settlers. By June 1825 the first tribes were being moved from their lands. In the next fifteen years all the remaining tribes were also bribed, persuaded or forced to go. The removal caused much misery to many Indians. The Cherokees came to call their journey west 'The Trail of Tears' because a quarter of their tribe died on the way.

Indian Territory and Indian Country

A section of land in the south west corner of the Great Plains, in present day Oklahoma, was set aside for these Eastern Indian tribes. It was called Indian Territory. A Bureau of Indian Affairs was set up in 1832 to look after the interests of the Indians. In 1834 the whole area of the Great Plains was set aside as Indian Country for 'as long as the stars shall shine and the rivers flow'.

1840-1851 'One Big Reservation'

In 1840 the United States government regarded the Great Plains as 'One Big Reservation'. In other words it was country where Indian tribes could wander

BELOW: *The Trail of Tears* by Robert Lindneux

freely wherever they wished in search of buffalo. The government had granted these lands to the Indians, but they were not motivated by any feelings of kindness. The lands were given to the Indians because the government believed no white men would ever want them. A frontier was drawn which the United States government thought no white man would ever wish to cross.

The first white men enter Indian Country

Yet within ten years of the declaration of the Permanent Indian Frontier white men had begun to cross the hunting grounds of the Plains Indians. It is true that they did not yet wish to settle on the plains. They were bound for the gold fields of California, the Willamette valley of Oregon, or the Mormon settlement in the Salt Lake Basin. But by 1850 deep wagon ruts marked the trails which these emigrants had made across the Indian lands. There were also many crosses by the side of these trails. These marked the graves of the travellers who died during Indian attacks on wagon trains. Many Indian tribes had become very hostile towards these travellers who crossed their hunting grounds and disturbed their buffalo (sources 102, 103).

It was not long before the government began to receive demands and pleas from traders and would-be emigrants. They wanted the government to find some way of protecting them against Indian attacks on their journey to California and Oregon.

ABOVE: Indian hunter orders the leader of a wagon train to retreat

SOURCE 102 'The Sioux Indian', extracts from a song about an Indian attack on a Mormon emigrant train

We crossed the Missouri and joined a larger train,
Which bore us o'er mountains and valleys and plains,
And often of an evening out hunting we'd go
To shoot the fleet antelope and the wild buffalo.

We heard of Sioux Indians all out on the plains,
A-killing poor drivers and burning their trains,
A-killing poor drivers with arrows and bows
When captured by Indians, no mercy they'd show.

Lomax, *Penguin Book of American Folk Songs*, p. 100

Gentlemen:

It being made my duty, to give instructions to emigrants to this territory, in regard to their conduct towards the natives, allow me to say that the Indians on the old road to this country, are friendly to the whites. They should be treated with kindness on all occasions. As Indians are inclined to steal, keep them out of your camps. It is best to keep in good sized companies while passing through their country. Small parties are sometimes stripped of their property while on their way to this Territory, perhaps because a preceding party promised to pay the Indians for something had of them, and failed to fulfil their promise. This will show you the necessity of keeping your word with them in all cases.

Dated at Oregon City this 22nd of April, 1847.

    Geo. Abernethy,

    Governor of Oregon Territory and Superintendent of Indian Affairs.

Benjamin Capps, *The Indians*, Time Life Inc., 1973, p. 132

1850-1867 The frontier begins to crumble: a policy of 'concentration'

By 1850 the US government was already having to think again about the idea of a Permanent Indian Frontier. The plains were no longer a region out at the end of nowhere. Nor were they needed as protection for the American states against the Mexicans. The war with the Mexicans ended in 1848 and the United States gained a large area of land in the South West. California and Oregon were attracting large numbers of settlers. Indian Country was now a barrier dividing the two coasts of America.

The government felt that the Indians could no longer be allowed to roam freely over the plains, attacking travellers on their way to these new and distant American lands. It therefore decided to make changes in the plan for an Indian homeland.

The meeting at Fort Laramie in 1851

In the autumn of 1851 a meeting took place between representatives of the government and the Indian tribes at Fort Laramie. The man who suggested the meeting and the place was Thomas Fitzpatrick. He had lived for many years in the Rocky Mountains as a trapper and in 1848 became Indian agent for the tribes in the region of the Arkansas, Platte and Kansas rivers. Fitzpatrick was deeply concerned about both Indians and white men. Year by year he had seen the slaughter of buffalo by the emigrants. He knew the effects of this and of white men's diseases (such as cholera) on the Indians (source 104). He knew that tribes like the Cheyenne were beginning to attack wagon trains. He feared that the time would soon come when a large scale Indian war would break out. This would bring great harm to both white men and Indians.

Fitzpatrick must have been greatly respected by the Indians. In September 1851 the greatest number of Indians ever gathered in one place, pitched their tepees at Horse Creek, fifty-six kilometres east of Fort Laramie.

SOURCE 104 Extract from Thomas Fitzpatrick's final report to the Bureau of Indian Affairs 1853, describing the effects of the traffic along the Oregon Trail on the Indians

They [the Plains Indians] are in want of food half the year. The travel upon the road drives the buffalo off. Their women are pinched with want and their children are constantly crying with hunger.

Ralph K. Andrist, *The Long Death*, Macmillan, 1964, p. 22

A policy of 'concentration'

It was little short of a miracle that so many old enemies came together in peace at this time. Just as amazing was the fact that the Plains Indians agreed to all the government's proposals (source 105). It seemed like a fair deal for both sides, though in fact the government gained most. It skilfully succeeded in changing the policy of one big reservation to a policy of concentration. This new policy aimed at restricting each Plains Indian tribe to a defined hunting ground. This, it was thought, would prevent the tribes warring amongst themselves and also help to protect travellers on the western trails.

The chiefs were told that once their lands were defined, they could live there for all time. Little did they realise that once their territories were marked out, it would be easier for the US government to force one tribe to give up its lands without arousing the anger of others.

LEFT: Fort Laramie by Alfred Jacob Miller

ABOVE: Night attack on a wagon train

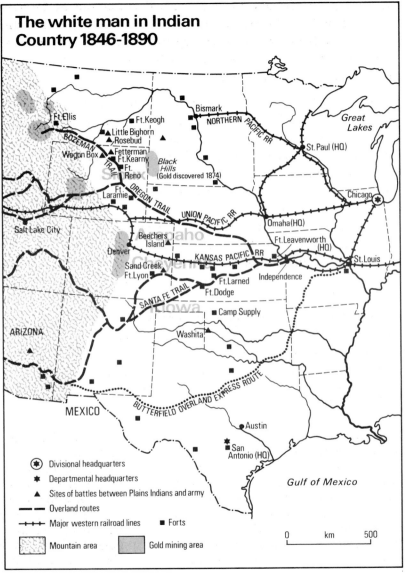

The white man in Indian Country 1846-1890

Ft. Ellis

Ft. Keogh

Bismark

NORTHERN PACIFIC RR

Great Lakes

Little Bighorn
Rosebud

BOZEMAN TRAIL

Wagon Box
Fetterman
Ft. Kearny

Black Hills
(Gold discovered 1874)

St. Paul (HQ)

Ft. Reno

OREGON TRAIL

Ft. Laramie

UNION PACIFIC RR

Chicago

Salt Lake City

Omaha (HQ)

Ft. Leavenworth (HQ)

Beechers Island

KANSAS PACIFIC RR

St. Louis

Denver

Independence

Sand Creek
Ft. Lyon

Ft. Larned

Ft. Dodge

SANTA FE TRAIL

Camp Supply

ARIZONA

Washita

BUTTERFIELD OVERLAND EXPRESS ROUTE

Austin

MEXICO

San Antonio (HQ)

Gulf of Mexico

✸ Divisional headquarters

★ Departmental headquarters

▲ Sites of battles between Plains Indians and army

━ ━ Overland routes

┼┼┼ Major western railroad lines

■ Forts

0 km 500

Mountain area   Gold mining area

SOURCE 105 Articles of a treaty made at Fort Laramie by Commissioners specially appointed by the President of the United States, and the chiefs, headmen and braves of the following Indian nations, viz, the Sioux, Cheyennes, Arapahos, Crows, Assiniboines, Gros-Ventres, Mandans and Arrickaras, 17 September 1851

Article 1: The Indian nations to make an effective and lasting peace.

Article 2: The Indian nations do hereby recognise the right of the United States government to establish roads, military and other posts, within their territories.

Article 3: The United States bind themselves to protect the Indian nations against all depredations by the people of the United States.

Article 5: The aforesaid Indian nations do . . . acknowledge the following tracts of country as their territories, viz:

The Territory of the Sioux Nation, commencing the mouth of the White Earth River; thence to the forks of the Platte River; thence up the north fork of the Platte River; thence along the range of mountains known as the Black Hills, to the head-waters of Heart River; thence down Heart River down the Missouri River to the place of beginning.

[descriptions of the territories of other tribes are omitted]

Article 7: The United States bind themselves to deliver to the Indian nations the sum of fifty thousand dollars per annum for the term of ten years in provisions, merchandise, domestic animals, and agricultural implements.

C. J. Kappler, *Indian Treaties 1778-1883*, (originally *Indian Affairs, Laws and Treaties*, Vol. 2 ,1904), Interland Publishing Inc, 1972, pp. 594-6

A fragile peace

The peace which was agreed on at Fort Laramie lasted only three years. The first incidents which broke the peace were in fact fairly trivial misunderstandings between wagon trains of emigrants and bands of Indians. By 1858 the Indians were becoming increasingly hostile to the overland mail coaches which now set out twice a week across the plains for California.

By 1860, however, a far more serious threat came to the Indian hunting grounds —that of white settlers on the plains and mountain fringes. The first of these were the farmers who began to move onto Indian lands in Kansas and Nebraska after 1854. Then in 1859 gold was discovered

ABOVE: Miners in Denver, during the Colorado 'gold rush'

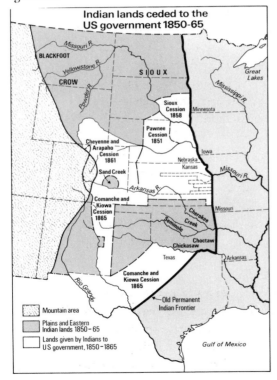

Indian lands ceded to the US government 1850-65

BLACKFOOT
Missouri R.
Yellowstone R.
CROW
Powder R.
SIOUX
Great Lakes
Mississippi R.
Sioux Cession 1858
Minnesota
Pawnee Cession 1851
Cheyenne and Arapaho Cession 1861
Iowa
Nebraska
Kansas
Sand Creek
Arkansas R.
Missouri
Comanche and Kiowa Cession 1865
Cherokee
Missouri
Seminole
Creek
Choctaw
Chickasaw
Texas
Arkansas
Comanche and Kiowa Cession 1865
Rio Grande
Old Permanent Indian Frontier

Mountain area

Plains and Eastern Indian lands 1850-65

Lands given by Indians to US government, 1850-1865

Gulf of Mexico

in the hills of Colorado. By the end of the year 25 000 miners had made their way across Indian lands to the gold fields in the Rockies. Thousands more were to follow.

The government was soon faced not only with the cries of travellers across the plains but also the demands of the settlers. The miners and cattlemen on the western edges of the plains and the farmers on the eastern began to call for the removal of the Indians (source 106). Their pleas were supported by the railroad companies who wanted to build a line across the plains to link east and west coasts. Railroad surveyors were already out on the plains. Stories of the 'iron horse' which would bring more settlers and frighten away the buffalo led to threats of war from Indian tribes.

SOURCE 106 Extract from a report written by the white agent of the Osage Indians in Kansas in 1864 to the Secretary of the Interior

The Indian lands are the best in the State, and justice would demand that these fertile lands should be thrown open to settlement and the abode of civilized and industrious men.

Report of Secretary of Interior, 1864, p. 536; in R. M. Robbins, *Our Landed Heritage*, University of Nebraska Press, 1961, p. 232

The Cheyenne on the warpath

The Cheyenne and the Arapaho were the first Plains Indian tribes to go on the warpath against the white men. They lived in the central area of the plains where the miners, traders, travellers and railroad men first made their intruding presence felt (see map, p. 120).

In February 1861, the government called the chiefs to a conference and forced them to give up all the lands granted to them at Fort Laramie in 1851. In return they were to have a small reservation between the Arkansas River and Sand Creek. For many warriors this was too much to take. They renounced the chiefs who had signed the treaty and went on the warpath through Colorado and New Mexico. For three years Cheyennes and Arapahos raided mining camps and settlers' homes, and destroyed mail coaches and overland mail stations.

Chivington's revenge: the Sand Creek Massacre

In 1864, when the Indians finally began to seek peace, the Coloradans took their revenge on the Indians. The local militia led by Colonel John Chivington attacked the camp of Black Kettle and his band of peaceful Cheyennes at Sand Creek. Within a few hours the battered corpses of Indians covered the ground (sources 107, 108, 109, 110).

SOURCE 107 A recruiting poster for the Colorado volunteers, a group of local militia who attacked Black Kettle's camp at Sand Creek, November 1864

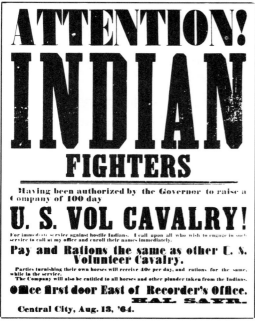

By courtesy of Colorado State Historical Society

The miners of Colorado paid dearly for their 'victory'. The Cheyennes and Arapahos retaliated with fury (source 111). The fear of the advance of railroads across the plains further added to the anger of the Indians (source 112).

SOURCE 108 Colonel Chivington's orders to the men who attacked Black Kettle's camp at Sand Creek in November 1864

Kill and scalp all, big and little; nits make lice.
Andrist, *The Long Death*, p. 89

SOURCE 109 Three conflicting accounts of the Sand Creek Massacre (November 1864): given as evidence to a military commission

The testimony of Major E. W. Wynkoop, US Army

From evidence of officers at this post, I understand that on 28th November, 1864, Colonel J. M. Chivington, with the third regiment of Colorado cavalry (one hundred days' men) attacked the camp of friendly Indians, the major portion of which were composed of women and children. Every one whom I have spoken to agrees that the most fearful atrocities were committed; women and children were killed and scalped; children shot at their mothers' breast, and all the bodies mutilated in the most horrible manner. Numerous eye-witnesses have described scenes to me of the most disgusting and horrible character; the dead bodies of females profaned in such a manner that the recital is sickening; Colonel J. M. Chivington all the time inciting his troops to these diabolical outrages. Knowing that these Indians had been promised protection by myself and Major S. J. Anthony, he kept his command in ignorance of this.

Colonel Chivington reports that between 500-600 Indians were left dead on the field. I have been informed by Captain Booth that he visited the field and counted 69 bodies. . . .

Extract from the testimony of Stephen Decatur, Colorado cavalryman

The next day after the battle. . . . I went over the battle-ground, and counted 450 dead Indian warriors. I saw something which made me feel as though I should have liked to have spent a little more time fighting. I saw some of the men opening bundles or bales. I saw them take therefrom a number of white persons' scalps—men's, women's

ABOVE: Colonel Chivington

BELOW: *Attack at dawn* by Charles Schreyvogel

and children's; I saw one scalp of a white woman in particular. The head had been skinned, taking all the hair; the scalp had been tanned to preserve it; the hair was auburn and hung in ringlets; it was very long hair.

Senate Executive Document 26, 39th Congress 2nd session, 1945, pp. 123-4: in Richmond and Mardock, *A Nation Moving West*, pp. 248-50

Extract from the testimony of Lieutenant Cramer

It was a mistake that there was any white scalps found in the village. I saw one but it was very old, the hair being much faded.

Reports of Committees of the 39th Congress, 2nd Session No. 156 pp. 73-4; in V. P. DeSantis, *America Past & Present*, Allyn and Bacon, 1968, p. 142

SOURCE 110 Verdict of the 'Denver News' on the Sand Creek Massacre

All acquitted themselves well. Colorado soldiers have again covered themselves with glory.

SOURCE 111 Report from the 'Miners' Register', Central City, 1865

We have just learned that Mr. Payne's train consisting of 50 wagons were attacked at daylight this morning. All the wagons were burned, 12 men killed. Also, some emigrants camped a few miles below here have been murdered. The telegraph office at Valley Station was almost annihilated.

The Legislature is now in session and we shall urge upon them the absolute necessity of offering rewards for Indian scalps, to be varied according to age and sex of the persons killed. It is only folly to talk about inhumanity and barbarity in dealing with these savages. There has always been a great mistake made in dealing with Indians. In war they should be dealt with as we deal with venomous reptiles. A war against them should be waged for their extermination.

Colorado Prospector, Vol. IV, No. 7, p. 3

SOURCE 112 A warning from Roman Nose, a Cheyenne Chief, to General Palmer in 1866

We will not have the wagons which make a noise [steam engines] in the hunting grounds of the buffalo. If the palefaces come further into our land there will be scalps of your brethren in the wigwams of the Cheyennes. I have spoken.

Charles H. L. Johnson, *Famous Indian Chiefs*, L. C. Page, 1909, p. 380

ABOVE: Indians attacking a stage coach

Red Cloud's War

Soon after the Sand Creek massacre the Sioux, who lived in the country to the north of Cheyenne lands, also went on the warpath. If you look at the map on p. 120 you will be able to understand why. We shall be studying this war (known as Red Cloud's War after the leading Sioux Chief) in more detail in one of our Case Studies. All we need say here is that the war against the Sioux went badly for the US army. By the spring of 1867 the soldiers in Sioux country were almost prisoners in their own forts. The Indian wars on the plains had become a serious matter.

1867-1875 A new problem and a new policy: Small Reservations

The new Indian Problem

The American government was greatly worried by the Sioux victories in autumn and spring of 1866-7. It made them realise that they had a new and even greater Indian problem on their hands. This time it was The Plains Indian Problem.

In 1840 the government had tried to solve the problems of conflicts between Indians and white men by giving the Indians land far away from white settlers, land which no white man would want.

Now, twenty years later, the white men had changed their minds. Indian lands contained gold for the miner. Some parts, in Kansas, Nebraska and Dakota, could be used by farmers. By 1867 men like Charles Goodnight and John Iliffe had also realised that the Indian hunting grounds were good for grazing cattle.

Faced with increasing pressure from miners, farmers and cattlemen what was the US government to do? There was no longer an easy solution to this problem. The Plains Indians would not be willing to give up their lands without a fierce fight. They were also very good fighters. Their skill as horsemen, their detailed knowledge of the countryside and their bravery made them deadly opponents. Moreover the Indians no longer had to rely only on bows and arrows as weapons. They now had guns supplied both by white traders and the Indian Bureau. Ironically the Indian Bureau provided these weapons for hunting buffalo not soldiers! But even if the Indians were defeated, what was to be done with them? There was no longer a Great American Desert to move Indians to, as the government had done before. Senator Lot Morill clearly set out the problem facing the government in a speech to the senate at this time. Here are some of his words:

SOURCE 113

We have come to the point in the history of the country that there is no place beyond the population to which you can remove the Indian, and the precise question is will you exterminate him or will you fix an abiding place for him?

Extermination or reservations?

The question of what to do with the Plains Indians split opinion into two opposing groups. One group, 'the humanitarians', wanted the Indians to be given a small amount of land and taught to 'walk the whiteman's road'. This meant learning to read and write and to make a living by farming instead of hunting (source 114).

Their opponents were the people who wanted the Indians to be wiped out entirely. This group of 'hardliners' was made up of army men, soldiers and officers, and also frontiersmen—the cattlemen, farmers and miners who had faced the Indian attacks. They agreed with General Philip Sheridan when he said 'The only good Indians I ever saw were dead' (source 115).

SOURCE 114 Extract from a letter written by Bishop H. B. Whipple of Minnesota to the American President in the early 1870s

On one side of the line [the boundary between USA and Canada] is a nation [the US] that has spent $500 000 000 in Indian wars. On the other [side] of the line are the Canadians (the same greedy, dominant Anglo-Saxon race) and the same heathen. They have not spent one dollar in Indian wars, and have had no Indian massacres. Why? In Canada the Indian treaties call these men 'the Indian subjects of Her Majesty'. When civilisation approaches them they are placed on ample reservations, receive aid in civilisation, have personal rights in property, are amenable to law, and protected by law, have schools and Christian people send them the best teachers. We expend more than $100 to their $1 in caring for Indian wards.

Dodge, *Hunting Grounds of the Great West*, p. xliii

SOURCE 115 The hardliners' view of the Indians:
General William Tecumseh Sherman, 1868, Military Chief on the High Plains

The more we can kill this year, the less will have to be killed next year. For the more I see of these Indians, the more convinced I am that all have to be killed or maintained as paupers.

Andrist, *The Long Death*, p. 154

BELOW: General Sherman

President Grant's peace policy

At first, the humanitarians won. The hard fact was that it cost two million dollars a year to keep an Indian fighting regiment in the plains. At this price it was cheaper to keep the Indians alive on reservations than to pay soldiers to kill them off.

President Grant decided to move the Indians from their allotted hunting grounds on to small reservations. These reservations were to be sited in areas of the plains where the white man still did not want to settle. This was land which was thought to have no gold or minerals, or to be too dry, barren or hilly for farming or cattle ranching.

The Medicine Lodge Creek meeting, October 1867

By the autumn of 1867 the southern tribes, the Cheyennes, Arapahos, Comanches and Kiowas were ready for peace. The peace commissioners were appointed. They loaded a wagon train with gifts and money, food, clothing, and other supplies and went off to meet the chiefs at Medicine Lodge Creek in Southern Kansas. Here new treaties were signed between white men and Indians. The chiefs agreed to give up their old hunting grounds and move on to small reservations in Indian Territory in the south east corner of the plains. Their speeches, however, show that some chiefs knew only too well what this new life would mean for the Plains Indians (sources 116, 117).

In November 1868 the commissioners negotiated a separate treaty with the Sioux at Fort Laramie. Red Cloud was the only Indian chief to gain anything from these new treaties. He was allowed to keep his old hunting grounds in the Black Hills of Dakota as his reservation.

BELOW: The Peace Commission at Medicine Lodge Creek, October 1867

SOURCE 116 Articles of a treaty entered into at Medicine Lodge Creek in the State of Kansas, by the United States of America (represented by its Commissioners), and the tribes of Kiowa and Comanche Indians (represented by their chiefs)

Article 4 The United States agrees to construct the following buildings: a warehouse and residence for the agent, a residence for the physician; and five other buildings, for a carpenter, farmer, blacksmith, miller and engineer; also a school-house or mission-building.

Article 8 The head of a family shall be entitled to receive seeds and agricultural implements. Such persons as commence farming shall receive instruction from a farmer.

Article 10 The United States agrees to deliver at the agency-house on the reservation, on the fifteenth day of October of each year, for thirty years, the following articles:

For each male person over fourteen years of age, a coat, pantaloons, flannel shirt, hat and a pair of home-made socks. For each female over twelve years of age, a flannel skirt, a pair of woollen hose, and twelve yards of calico.

Article 11 The tribes further agree:

1st. That they will withdraw all opposition to the construction of the railroad now being built on the Smoky Hill River. . . .

3rd. That they will not attack any persons at home, nor travelling, nor disturb any wagon trains, coaches, mules or cattle.

Kappler, *Indian Treaties 1778-1883*, pp. 977-982

SOURCE 117 Extract from a speech made by Ten Bears, a Comanche Chief, at Medicine Lodge in October 1867

My heart is filled with joy when I see you here, as the brooks fill with water when the snow melts in the spring.

But there are things you have said to me which were not sweet like sugar, but bitter like gourds. You said that you wanted to put us upon a reservation and to build us houses. I do not want them. I was born upon the prairie where the wind blew free and there was nothing to break the light of the sun.

When I was at Washington, the Great Father told me that all Comanche land was ours and that no one should hinder us in living upon it. So why do you ask us to leave the rivers and the sun and the wind and live in houses? Do not ask us to give up the buffalo for the sheep. The young men have heard talk of this and it has made them sad and angry.

W. C. Vanderwerth, *Indian Oratory: Famous Speeches by Noted Indian Chieftains*,

© 1971 by the University of Oklahoma Press. This extract quoted from Ballantine Books, 1972, pp. 130-1

BELOW: Ten Bears: a Comanche Chief

War breaks out yet again

The peace lasted less than a year. By the end of 1868 fighting had broken out once again. There were faults on both sides. The US government wrongly assumed that because the treaties were signed by a few chiefs (many of whom were old, weary or corrupt) that the rest of the tribes would accept the terms. Not so. Most young warriors were not willing to give up their hunting grounds in favour of a few acres and a plough. They refused to remain within the narrow confines of their reservations. The government added to the problem by failing to provide a decent life on many Indian reservations (source 118). Young warriors took to fighting as well as hunting (source 119) and the army chiefs continued to press for an extermination policy.

Attitudes on both sides hardened (source 120). The southern tribes were the first to go on the warpath. Chief Black Kettle of the Cheyennes was anxious to avenge the attack on his village at Sand Creek. In August of 1868 he led his warriors through Kansas attacking and burning settlements as they went. His raids inspired other tribes—Kiowas, Arapahos, Comanches and Apaches—to join them on the warpath. By the end of the year, two thousand warriors were roving the plains from Kansas to Texas. Railroads as well as wagon trains, cattlemen and farmers were attacked this time.

ABOVE: Indians attacking navvies on the Union Pacific Railroad

SOURCE 118 A description of the food given to the Indians on the Crow-Creek Reservation, 1863-1864

The greatest evil is that the Indians are poorly clothed and badly fed or starved, and unless they are so degraded as to have lost all spirit they make trouble. I doubt if there is a reservation in the country on which the average white labouring man would be content to live and subsist on Indian rations. Take this description of the fare at Crow-Creek Agency in 1863-64:

'Some time about the middle of the winter into a large vat, about six feet [2 m] square and six feet [2 m] deep were thrown beef, beef heads, entrails of beeves, some beans, flour and pork. This mass was then cooked by the steam. When that was done all the Indians were ordered to come there with their pails and get it. It was about the consistency of very thin gruel. Some of the Indians refused to eat it, saying they could not eat it, it made them sick. They told the agent that it was only fit for hogs, and they were not hogs. The Indians reported several deaths from starvation; they were constantly begging for something to eat.'

This was the testimony of S. C. Haynes, assistant surgeon of the Sixth Iowa Cavalry. Even worse was proven, for it was shown that beeves were used that had died natural deaths, and that meat was issued which stank and was full of maggots.

J. P. Dunn, *Massacres of the Mountains* (1886), Eyre and Spottiswoode Frontier Library, 1963, pp. 26-7

SOURCE 119 A Comanche and Kiowa raid on Charles Goodnight's cattle in the Palo Duro Canyon, Colorado

All went well until the fall of 1878 when a large band of Indians left the Territorial Reserves and headed back into Texas, ostensibly upon a buffalo hunt. They passed Fort Elliot and struck into the canyons of the Palo Duro. Disappointed at not finding game, and having many hungry mouths to feed, the Indians found and began killing JA [ranch] cattle.

'The line riders on the east side sent me a runner,' said Goodnight, 'stating that Indians were coming in considerable numbers. I at once mounted a good horse and started to meet them.'

'Don't you know this country is ours?' one [Indian] asked.

'What are you doing here?' and every face was on me.

'Raising cattle.'

'Aren't you killing buffaloes?'

'No'.

'Aren't you killing them to eat?'

'No. I have plenty of fat cattle, and buffaloes aren't much good.'

'What have you got to offer?' they asked.

'I've got plenty of guns and plenty of bullets, good men and good shots, but I don't

ABOVE: Chief Gall of the Hunkpapa Sioux

BELOW: Charles Goodnight's ranch

want to fight unless you force me.' Then, pointing to Quanah (Quanah Parker the half breed Comanche Chief) I said, 'You keep order, and behave yourself, protect my property and let it alone, and I'll give you two beeves every other day until you find out where the buffaloes are.'

And so they treated and settled down together in perfect peace. The cowman kept his word in regard to the beeves and Quanah—? Goodnight says he never knew an Indian who failed to keep his.

Haley, *Charles Goodnight*, pp. 306–8

SOURCE 120 The views of an Indian and a white man who were not in favour of the peace policy

General William Tecumseh Sherman: Military Chief on the High Plains September 1868

We have now selected and provided reservations for all off the great road. All who cling to their old hunting grounds are hostile and will remain so till killed off.

Andrist, *The Long Death*, p. 154

Gall, Chief of the Hunkpapa Sioux, 1868

You fought me and I had to fight back: I am a soldier. The annuities you speak of we don't want. Our intention is to take no presents. You talk of peace. If we make peace, you will not hold it. My people told me to get powder and ball, and I want that.

W. C. Vanderwerth, *Indian Oratory: Famous Speeches by Noted Indian Chieftains*, © 1971 by the University of Oklahoma Press. This extract quoted from Ballantine Books, 1972, pp. 150–1

The army takes command

The Indian raids played straight into the army's hands. Peaceful persuasion did not work, they said. They felt it was time for the army to step in and crush the Indians once and for all.

They began to use a new strategy in the war against the Indians—the winter campaign. Previously the army had fought the Indians in the summer. This was because the summer was the best time for war—when the grass was green and horses were well fed. Now they began to attack the winter camps of the tribes, striking not only at the warriors but also at their wives and children. They burnt their tepees and their clothes, took their food and shot their ponies.

The first successful battle in this campaign was the Battle of the River Washita.

ABOVE: Custer in his civil war uniform as Major-General

ABOVE: The Battle of the Washita

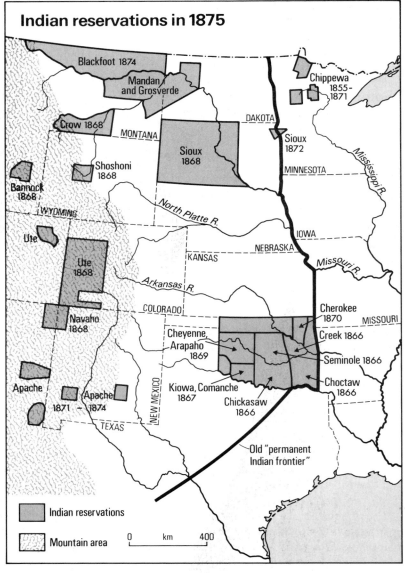

Indian reservations in 1875

Blackfoot 1874

Mandan and Grosverde

Chippewa 1855-1871

Crow 1868

MONTANA

DAKOTA

Sioux 1872

Sioux 1868

Mississippi R.

MINNESOTA

Shoshoni 1868

Bannock 1868

WYOMING

North Platte R.

IOWA

Ute

Missouri R.

NEBRASKA

Ute 1868

KANSAS

Arkansas R.

Navaho 1868

COLORADO

Cherokee 1870

MISSOURI

Cheyenne, Arapaho 1869

Creek 1866

Seminole 1866

Apache

Apache 1871 — 1874

NEW MEXICO

Kiowa, Comanche 1867

Chickasaw 1866

Choctaw 1866

TEXAS

Old "permanent Indian frontier"

Indian reservations

Mountain area

0   km   400

Colonel George Armstrong Custer and his cavalry attacked the winter camp of Black Kettle and his Cheyennes. Black Kettle was killed and the fighting spirit of his tribe was broken. The other tribes fought on for six years before they were defeated and sent back to their reservation. Between 1875 and 1876 the Sioux also went to war once again. In the end they too were forced to give in.

The defeat of the Plains Indians

There were many reasons for the defeat of the Plains Indians. We shall look at these in more detail in our Case Study about the Sioux. The most important single cause, however, was the virtual destruction of the buffalo between 1867 and 1883 (source 121). First they were killed by emigrants and railroadmen for food. By 1870 however, the 'sportsmen' had moved in. They were followed by the professional hunter (source 122). Without a food supply no army can continue to fight indefinitely. The Plains Indians were no exception.

SOURCE 121 **Figures showing the buffalo hides and meat handled by the Railroad Companies, 1872-74**

Years	Hides delivered	Dead Buffalo
1872	497 163	1 491 489
1873	754 329	1 508 658
1874	126 867	158 583
	1 378 359	3 158 730

Dodge, *Hunting Grounds of the Great West*, p. 140

ABOVE: The buffalo hunters

SOURCE 122 Two white men's views of the killing of the buffalo

General Philip Sheridan, US Army

These men [the buffalo hunters] have done [more] in the last two years, and will do more in the next year, to settle the vexed Indian question, than the entire regular army has done in the last thirty years. They are destroying the Indians' commissary; and it is a well-known fact that an army losing its base of supplies is placed at a great disadvantage. Send them powder and lead, if you will; but, for the sake of a lasting peace, let them kill, skin, and sell until the buffaloes are exterminated. Then your prairies can be covered with speckled cattle, and the festive cowboy, [the] forerunner of an advanced civilisation.

John R. Cook, *The Border and the Buffalo*, Lakeside Press, 1938, p. 164

Teddy Blue Abbot, a cowboy in the 1880s

That buffalo slaughter was a dirty business. They would have two skinners working with each pair of hunters and the hunters would round up a bunch of buffalo and shoot all down they could. The skinners would follow after in a wagon and take the hides. But when it got dark they would quit, leaving maybe ten or twenty carcasses. Next spring they would just lie there on the prairie and rot, hides and all. It was all waste. All this slaughter was a put up job on the part of the government to control Indians by getting rid of their food supply. But just the same it was a low down dirty business.

E. C. Abbott and Helena Huntington Smith, *We Pointed Them North*, University of Oklahoma Press, 1966, p. 101

The vanishing Americans: Indian life 1875-1895

Life on the reservations

By 1885 the last of the defeated warriors were chased back to the reservations. There, finally, they were forced to stay.

Once there were no more buffalo to hunt the Indians had no choice but to sit and wait for their government rations. Life on the reservation weakened many Indians in spirit and in body. The numbers in many tribes dwindled rapidly (source 123).

LEFT: Ration day at Pine Ridge Sioux reservation in the 1880s

SOURCE 123 Two views of the effects of reservation life on the Indians

Geronimo, sub-chief of the Apache Indians, comments on life on an Oklahoma reservation after 1877

We are now held on Comanche and Kiowa lands, which are not suited to our needs. Our people are decreasing in numbers here, and will continue to decrease unless they are allowed to return to their native land. There is no climate or soil which is equal

ABOVE: Apaches in Arizona

to that of Arizona. We would have plenty of good cultivating land, plenty of grass, plenty of timber and plenty of minerals in that land which the Almighty created for the Apaches. I want to spend my last days there, and be buried among those mountains. If this could be I might die in peace, feeling that my people, placed in their native homes, would increase in numbers, rather than diminish as at present and that our name would not become extinct.

Barrett, *Geronimo*, pp. 170-3

George Bird Grinnell describes Pawnee life on a reservation in Oklahoma

During the first four years of their stay in the Indian Territory [Oklahoma] the condition of the Pawnees was most miserable.

The wretched condition of the Pawnees continued up to about 1884 or 1885. By then they had come to realise that it was absolutely necessary for them to go to work if the tribe was to continue to exist. They began to work; at first only a few, but gradually many. Presently a point was reached where it was no longer necessary to issue them government rations. They raised enough on their farms to support themselves. Each year of late they have done better and better. Nowadays by far the greater number of Pawnees wear civilized clothing, ride in wagons and send their children to the agency school. They are making rapid strides toward civilization, just such progress as might be expected from the intelligent and courageous people that they are and always have been.

Pawnee Hero Stories and Folk Tales, Scribner, 1890, pp. 389-402, reprinted by University of Nebraska Press, 1961

The end of the tribal system

Moving the Indians to reservations did not completely solve the Indian problem. The government still thought that the Indians' great loyalty to their tribe, their chief and their way of life would cause trouble in the future. They therefore began a policy aimed at breaking down the Indians' loyalty to their tribe and chief. They hoped that the Indians would begin to think of themselves as individual white men. This policy had begun, in fact, in 1871 when the government refused to sign any more treaties with tribal chiefs. In the 1880s the Indian agents began to encourage members of each tribe to set up their own law courts and to ignore the powers of the chiefs. Then in 1885 the Indians' own law courts were abolished and the government gave the right of punishing the Indians to United States federal courts.

LEFT: An agency policeman by Frederic Remington

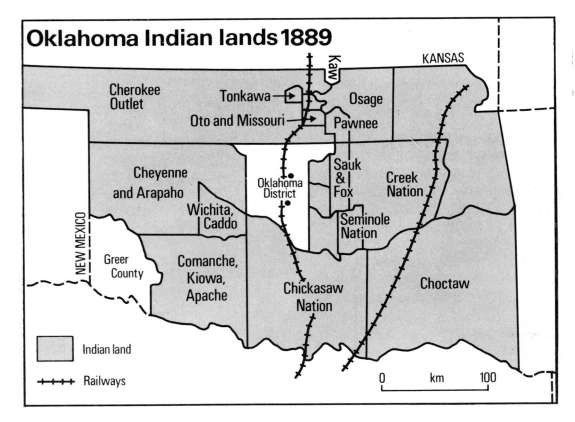

Oklahoma Indian lands 1889

KANSAS

NEW MEXICO

Cherokee Outlet

Tonkawa →

Oto and Missouri →

Kaw

Osage

Pawnee

Sauk & Fox

Creek Nation

Cheyenne and Arapaho

Oklahoma District

Wichita, Caddo

Seminole Nation

Greer County

Comanche, Kiowa, Apache

Chickasaw Nation

Choctaw

Indian land

+++++ Railways

0   km   100

The government also began to try to destroy the way of life of the Indians. In some ways they hoped that this would benefit the Indians. In particular, schools were set up to train the Indians in technical and agricultural subjects. In other ways it aimed to destroy the Indians' feeling of being a separate people so that they would fit more easily into the whiteman's way of life.

The final step was taken when in 1887 the President was given the power to divide up the lands of any tribe and give the head of each family one hundred and sixty acres for his own farm. There is no doubt that this benefited some Indian families. It also, however, provided an opening for those settlers who wished to move onto Indian lands—especially the millions of hectares which had been given to the twenty-two tribes in Indian Territory in the southeast of the plains.

The beginning of the end of Indian Territory

Since the beginning of the 1880s groups of farmers and other settlers had been moving into Indian Territory in the hope of staking their claims on land unoccupied by Indians. Time after time the government had brought in troops to move these settlers out. This went on for five years. Then farmers and railway companies began sending petitions to Congress demanding that Indian Territory be opened up to white settlers.

Finally, in 1885 farmers and railway men got their way. The government agreed to negotiate with the Creeks and Seminoles for two areas of their land which were still uninhabited: Cherokee Outlet and Oklahoma District. It took three years for an agreement to be reached. In January 1889 the Creeks and Seminoles handed over this land for a price of over four million dollars.

That day saw the beginning of the end of Indian Territory and the beginning of the state of Oklahoma. It had taken only fifty years for the government to take away most of the land they had promised the Indians 'for as long as the stars shall shine and the rivers flow'. Plains Indians had to suffer the same fate as the Eastern Indians (source 124). The day of the Plains Indians and of the buffalo had come to an end.

ABOVE: An Indian ploughing by Frederic Remington

SOURCE 124 An Indian view of the Red Man's fate, by a spokesman for the Choctaw and Chickasaw Nation, 1895

We ask every lover of justice, is it right that a great and powerful government should, year by year, continue to demand cessions of land from weaker and dependent people, under the plea of securing homes for the homeless. While the great government of the United States, our guardian, is year by year admitting foreign paupers into the Union, at the rate of 250 000 per annum, must we sacrifice our homes and children for this pauper element? They [the whiteman] care nothing for the fate of the Indian, so that their own greed can be gratified.

Answer to Report of the Honourable Dawes Commission by the Choctaw and Chickasaw Nations, Indian Pamphlets No. 7, in McLuhan, *Touch the Earth*, pp. 96-7

The Battle of the Little Bighorn

Introduction

It was early morning on 25 June 1876, when Colonel George Armstrong Custer, US 7th Cavalry, stood looking down onto the valley of the Little Bighorn River. It was already hazy with the rising heat of the day. Custer could hardly see what his scouts had warned him was there—the largest assembly of Indians ever to be faced by the US army. There were nearly 12 000 Indians—men, women and children from all the main Sioux bands and their Cheyenne and Arapaho allies. Of these, there were perhaps 2000 warriors and 20 000 ponies. 'The largest Indian camp on the North American continent is ahead', Custer had said on the previous night, 'and I am going to attack it'.

Custer had only 600 men. They had ridden 48 kilometres the day before in the burning heat and ten more during the night and were now resting without unsaddling. It was still at least 24 kilometres to the Indian village. Custer gave the order to advance.

Later, as they rode further down the valley and peered across the river, Custer could see the true size of the village for the first time. He waved his hat and yelled to his men, 'Courage boys, we have got them; the Indians are asleep in their tepees'. But this time he was wrong. That evening George Armstrong Custer and half of his men lay dead on the battlefield. The Sioux leaders Crazy Horse, Gall and Sitting Bull and their warriors had inflicted the worst defeat of the Indian wars on the US army. As the news spread, Americans everywhere were stunned. 'The announcement of the annihilation of Custer and this large body of men shocked the entire country', wrote General Miles. 'I remember reading on the morning of July 6 . . . the headline of a newspaper printed . . . across the entire page, the single word HORRIBLE.' People began to ask questions: how and why did this disaster happen?

In this case study we shall be looking at the Battle of the Little Bighorn or 'Custer's Last Stand' as it came to be known, and considering the following questions:

Why did such a battle take place at this time?

What happened at the Battle of the Little Bighorn?

Why were Custer and his men defeated and killed?

Was the Battle of the Little Bighorn really a victory for the Sioux?

A BLOODY BATTLE.

An Attack on Sitting Bull on the Little Horn River.

GENERAL CUSTER KILLED.

The Entire Detachment Under His Command Slaughtered.

SEVENTEEN OFFICERS SLAIN.

ABOVE LEFT: *Custer's last stand* by Kurz and Allison: one of the many imaginary reconstructions of the Battle
ABOVE: Headlines from the *New York Herald* 6 July 1876

The main bands of the Western Sioux nation

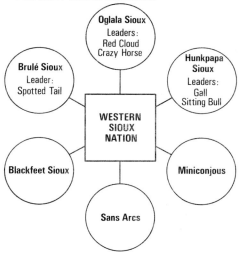

Mississippi River, and the western (or Teton) Sioux. It was the conflict between the western Sioux and the US government which led eventually to the Battle of the Little Bighorn.

By the 1840s the western Sioux had found rich hunting grounds in the high plains of Dakota and in the foothills of the Rockies in Montana and Wyoming. Until the 1860s however, there was little serious trouble between the Sioux and the whitemen. Only the southern bands, who hunted along the North Platte river, had been disturbed by wagon trains along the Oregon Trail.

The Bozeman Trail
Then in 1862 gold was discovered in the Rocky Mountains in Montana. In order to get supplies from the Oregon Trail to the goldfields, a miner named John Bozeman opened up a new trail which ran north west from the Platte river and along the eastern edge of the Bighorn Mountains.

Why did such a battle take place at this time?

The Sioux Indians
The Battle of the Little Bighorn came as the climax of many years of conflict and dispute between the US government and the Sioux Indians. The Sioux was one of the proudest and most powerful of the Indian nations. Like many of the Plains Indian tribes, they had been gradually pushed westward by the whitemen onto the Great Plains in the eighteenth century. By the 1850s the Sioux nation had become divided into two: the eastern Sioux, who remained near the Great Lakes and the

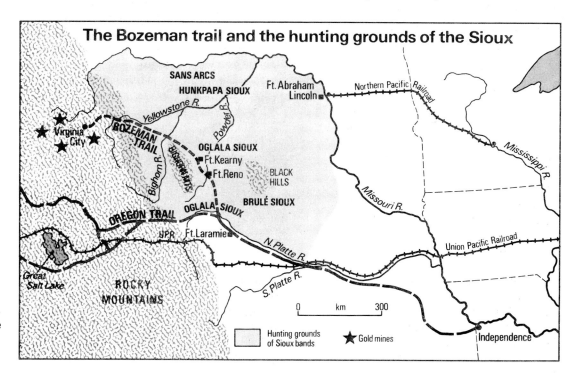

The Bozeman trail and the hunting grounds of the Sioux

It became known as the Bozeman Trail and it ran straight through the heart of the Sioux hunting grounds.

Unlike the Oregon Trail, the Bozeman Trail affected the lives of many of the Sioux bands. To the miners it was a vital route for their supplies. But the Sioux had a different attitude towards the Bozeman Trail as Black Elk, Holy Man of the Oglala Sioux, recalled:

SOURCE 125 Black Elk's view of the Bozeman Trail

I was born in the moon of the Popping Trees on the Little Power River in the winter when the four Crows [Crow Indians] were killed [1863]. When I was older, I learned what the fighting was about that winter and the next summer. The Wasichus [whitemen] had found much of the yellow metal that they worship and that makes them crazy and they wanted to have a road up through our country to the place where the yellow metal was. But my people did not want the road it would scare the bison [buffalo] and make them go away and also it would let the other Wasichus come in like a river. And so, when the soldiers came and built themselves a town of logs [Fort Reno], my people knew that they meant to have their road and take our country and maybe kill us all when they were strong enough. Crazy Horse was only 19 then and Red Cloud was still our Greatest Chief. In the Moon of the Changing Seasons [October] he called together all the scattered bands of the Lakota [Sioux] for a big council on the Powder River and . . . we went on the warpath against the soldiers.

Neihardt, *Black Elk Speaks*, pp. 18–19

For the next two years, Red Cloud and his Sioux warriors harassed travellers along the Bozeman Trail. They were so successful that in the summer of 1866, the US government arranged a council at Fort Laramie with Red Cloud and other Sioux leaders. The government hoped that they would be able to negotiate a peace so that travellers could use the trail as long as they did not disturb the buffalo. In the middle of the talks, however, Colonel Carrington arrived with a detachment of troops. They had orders to set up a chain of forts along the road to protect travellers against Indian raids. News of Carrington's orders soon reached Red Cloud. He immediately refused to continue the talks and left the Council with these words:

SOURCE 126

You are the White Eagle who has come to steal the road! The Great Father [the US President] sends us presents and wants us to sell him the road, but the White Chief comes with the soldiers to steal it before the Indian says yes or no. I will talk with you no more. I will go now and I will fight you! As long as I live I will fight you for the last hunting grounds of my people.

Senate Executive Document No. 33, US 50th Congress, 1st Session

Red Cloud's War

This was the start of Red Cloud's War. The campaign which followed was a victory for Red Cloud and other Sioux leaders, Crazy Horse and Sitting Bull. Colonel Carrington was able to establish two forts but his men soon found themselves besieged inside them. Then, in December 1866, Crazy Horse and his warriors wiped out a detachment of nearly one hundred soldiers under Captain W. Fetterman while they were on a wood cutting expedition.

By the spring of 1867 it became clear to the government that the forts could not be held and the Bozeman Trail defended without more men and more money. So the government in Washington sent offers of peace to Red Cloud and the other leaders. Red Cloud refused even to come and talk: 'We are in the mountains', he said, 'when we see the soldiers moving away and the forts abandoned, then I will come down to talk.'

Because they were not willing at this time to spend millions of dollars on yet another Indian war, the government had little choice. In July 1868 the troops withdrew and Red Cloud and his warriors burned the forts to the ground.

The Great Sioux Reservation

On 4 November 1868, Red Cloud rode into Fort Laramie to sign the peace treaty. By the terms of this agreement, Red Cloud and the chiefs and people of the Oglala, Brulé and Miniconjou bands agreed to move onto the vast Great Sioux Reservation. This was to cover all of South Dakota west of the Missouri. It also included the Black Hills which to the Sioux were a sacred and special place. In return, the Sioux were granted great concessions as these extracts from the peace treaty show:

FAR LEFT: Black Elk, Holy Man of the Oglala Sioux
LEFT: The Fetterman Massacre from *Harper's Weekly* 21 December 1866
ABOVE: Red Cloud of the Oglala Sioux

SOURCE 127

Article 2 The United States agrees that . . . all reservations should be set apart for the absolute and undisturbed use and occupation of the Sioux Indians . . . and the United States now solemnly agrees that no persons except . . . such officers, agents and employees of the government as may be authorised to enter upon Indian reservations, shall ever be permitted to pass over, settle upon, or reside in [this] territory.

Article 16 The United States hereby agrees . . . that the country north of the North Platte River and east of the summits of the Bighorn Mountains shall be . . . considered to be unceded Indian Territory, and also . . . agrees that no white persons shall be permitted to settle upon or occupy any portion of [it]; and it is further agreed by the United States, that within ninety days after the conclusion of peace with the Sioux Nation, the military posts now established in this territory shall be abandoned, and that the road leading to them and by them to the settlements in the Territory of Montana shall be closed.
Kappler, *Indian Treaties 1778–1883*, pp. 998, 1002–3

'I have more soldiers than the Great Father and he cannot take my lands against my will', commented Red Cloud after the signing of the treaty. At that moment Red

Cloud felt proud. He had fought the US army and won. As a result the Bozeman Trail was closed and the forts abandoned. The Sioux had been allowed to keep all of their hunting grounds and the sacred Black Hills. Red Cloud was the first and only western Indian Chief to win such a victory. After fighting and threats the Kiowa and Comanche, the Cheyenne and Arapaho had been forced to give up their hunting grounds and accept small, barren reservations in the south east of the plains. In the autumn of 1868 it seemed to Red Cloud that the lands of his people and their way of life were secure 'as long as the grass should grow and the water flow'.

Death of MacDonald, the mail carrier, from a drawing by Sitting Bull.

ABOVE: Sitting Bull kills a mail carrier (from his autobiography)
ABOVE RIGHT: George Armstrong Custer

The Problem of Sitting Bull and Crazy Horse

The treaty of 1868 did not work out as either Red Cloud or the US government had hoped. Many chiefs and their bands did indeed follow Red Cloud and the Oglala Sioux and agree to live on the reservation. Many other Sioux bands, however, like the Hunkpapas, the Sans Arcs and some Oglalas did not sign the treaty. They followed Crazy Horse and Sitting Bull who refused to give up their old way of life and live on a reservation. These 'wild Indians' continued to roam the Bighorn country in search of buffalo and to be hostile towards any whitemen who crossed their hunting grounds. They would keep the peace only as long as the whitemen kept the terms of the treaty and remained outside their land.

Gold and Custer in the Black Hills

Within six years of signing the treaty the US government had changed its mind about the lands they had given to the Sioux. Rumours began to circulate about gold finds in the Black Hills. In 1874, an army scouting expedition was sent out commanded by George Armstrong Custer. 'Long Hair' Custer was one of the army commanders most hated by the Plains Indians. He had a reputation as a ruthless Indian fighter. News of his attack on the peaceful village of Black Kettle and his Cheyennes in 1868 had spread far and wide among the Plains Indians.

Black Elk, Holy Man of the Oglala Sioux, later described the result of Custer's expedition in 1874:

SOURCE 128

It was when I was eleven years old [1874] that the first sign of new trouble came to us. Scouts came to us and said that many soldiers had come into the Black Hills. Afterwards I learned that it was Long Hair who had led his soldiers into the Black Hills that summer to see what he could find. He had no right to go there because all that country was ours.

ABOVE: Custer's expedition in the Black Hills

ABOVE: Deadwood City, a mining camp in the Black Hills which grew quickly in 1875 after Custer's expedition

Also the Wasichus had made a treaty with Red Cloud [1868] that said it would be ours as long as grass should grow and water flow. Later I learned too that Long Hair had found there much of the yellow metal that makes the Wasichus crazy, and that is what made the bad trouble just as it did before when the 100 were rubbed out. In the fall we heard that some Wasichus had come from the Missouri River to dig in the Black Hills for the yellow metal because Long Hair had told them about it with a voice that went everywhere. Later he got rubbed out for doing that.

Neihardt, *Black Elk Speaks*, pp. 62-3

How much to buy the Black Hills?
By 1875 a new gold rush had begun—this time to the Black Hills. Thousands of prospectors poured into the Sioux hunting grounds. At first the army tried to keep the miners out of the Black Hills. It was a hopeless task for there were too many of them. Next Red Cloud appealed to the President in Washington about this invasion of this reservation. But the government found it impossible either to keep the miners out, or protect them against Indian attacks. So, in the summer of 1875, the President decided to send a group of commissioners to negotiate with the Sioux for the purchase of the Black Hills. The commissioners had little success. Red Cloud calmly proposed a price of $600 000 000. Crazy Horse and Sitting Bull would not even meet the commissioners. 'One does not sell the earth upon which the people walk', Crazy Horse had said. Moreover, the Black Hills were sacred ground where warriors went to speak with the Great Spirit and await visions. 'The land known as the Black Hills is considered by the Indians as the centre of their land', said Running Antelope. He, like most of the Sioux Indians, was against selling the Black Hills at any price.

The commissioners then returned to Washington to report their failure. To many government officials the attitude of the Indians seemed quite unreasonable. Why were they so unwilling to sell this land to the whitemen who would, after all, be able to make good use of it? Many government officials were now becoming very impatient with the Sioux—especially the 'wild' bands of Crazy Horse and Sitting Bull who still roamed free in the Bighorn Mountains. They would never agree to sell the Black Hills. In the view of Indian Inspector E. C. Watkins, there was only one thing to be done about these Sioux bands, as he stated in his report to the Commissioner of Indian Affairs in 1875:

SOURCE 129
The true policy, in my judgement, is to send troops against them in winter, the sooner the better, and whip them into subjection. They richly merit punishment for their incessant warfare and their numerous murders of white settlers and their families, or whitemen wherever found unarmed.

Senate Executive Document No. 184, US 44th Congress, 1st Session, pp. 8-9

145

LEFT: Sitting Bull of the
Hunkpapa Sioux
BELOW: General Philip Sheridan

The Bighorn campaign

The Indian Commissioners first decided that the bands of Crazy Horse and Sitting Bull should be given a chance to come into the reservation of their own free will. Black Elk later recalled the message sent to his band:

SOURCE 130

During the winter [December 1875] runners came from the Wasichus and told us we must come into the soldiers' town [Fort Robinson] right away or there would be bad trouble. But it was foolish to say that, because it was very cold and many of our people and ponies would have died in the snow. Also we were in our own country and were doing no harm.

Neihardt, *Black Elk Speaks*, p. 70

By 31 January 1876 none of the roaming bands had come in. As a result they were declared 'hostile' and the army was given the job of dealing with them. General Philip Sheridan now made plans to round up or destroy the bands of Sitting Bull and Crazy Horse. Army scouts reported that they were in the Bighorn Mountains. This was a wild and rugged area and the Sioux would be hard to find and pin down. Sheridan, therefore, decided to send three army columns. These were to advance on the Bighorn Mountains from three directions. General Crook's column, moving north from Fort Fetterman, was the first to meet up with the Sioux on 17 June 1876. He fought a large band of warriors led by Crazy Horse. Although Crook's losses were not great, Crazy Horse stopped Crook's advance, and the General was forced to return to Fort Fetterman.

The road to Little Bighorn

The other two army columns met up as planned at a point on the Yellowstone River, north of the Bighorn Mountains. One column under Colonel Gibbon had marched east from Montana. The other, led by General Terry, had moved west from Fort Abraham Lincoln. As part of his force, General Terry had brought the 7th Cavalry. In command of the cavalry was none other than George Armstrong Custer. General Terry was now almost certain that the Sioux were in a summer camp in the valley of the stream known as the Little Bighorn. He therefore ordered Gibbon and the 7th Infantry to march south up the Little Bighorn. Meanwhile Custer and the fast-moving 7th Cavalry were ordered to make for the southern end of the Wolf mountains and then march north down the Little Bighorn. The timing of the movements of the two columns was vital. If they converged on the Indian camp at the same time then the Indians would be trapped. If one arrived too early then the Indians would have a chance to escape.

On 22 June 1876, Custer and the 7th Cavalry left camp on the Yellowstone River in search of the Sioux. Their camp was indeed where Terry had guessed it to be. But Terry was wrong about one thing—it was much larger than he expected. After Crook's battle with Crazy Horse, the

Sioux had realised that the army was on their trail. Crazy Horse and Sitting Bull had joined their forces and pitched camp together by the Little Bighorn river. Many other bands joined them including young warriors from Red Cloud's reservation and groups of Cheyenne and Arapaho. Most of the warriors were well armed. A camp of 12 000 Indians was unusual, but then so was the occasion. The Indians realised the danger to their land and their way of

life and were determined to make a stand. 'The whites want war,' Sitting Bull said, 'and we will give it them.'

What happened at the Battle of the Little Bighorn?

While the army columns were advancing towards them, the Sioux held a Sun Dance. Sitting Bull had danced for three days and in his trance he saw soldiers falling upside down into the Indian camp. This was a certain sign of an Indian victory. On 25 June George Armstrong Custer and his 7th Cavalry found the Indians in the valley of the Little Bighorn and fell into their camp just as Sitting Bull had prophesied.

Exactly what happened to Custer on that day we will never know. None of the men who fought alongside Custer survived to tell the story. Many people have since tried to piece together the events. One of them was John Finerty, war correspondent of the *Chicago Times*, who travelled with General Crook's army during the Bighorn campaign. He used the reports of the army investigation and the statements of Indians who fought that day to compile the following account of the Battle of the Little Bighorn.

The strategy of the Bighorn campaign

Ft. Shaw
Missouri R.
North Dakota
Montana
Yellowstone R.
Ft. Abraham Lincoln
Northern Pacific Railroad
GIBBON'S column
TERRY–CUSTER column
Bighorn R.
Battle of Little Bighorn, 25 June
Battle against Crazy Horse, 17 June
BIGHORN MTS
CROOK'S column
Powder R.
Deadwood
BLACK HILLS
Custer City
Missouri R.
ROCKY MOUNTAINS
Great Sioux Reservation granted by 1868 Treaty
Wyoming
Ft. Fetterman
Ft. Robinson
Nebraska
Ft. Laramie

Unceded Indian Country:
Indian hunting grounds where white men were forbidden to settle by the terms of the 1868 Treaty

0   km   100

SOURCE 131

The march to the Little Bighorn

[After taking leave of General Terry] Custer marched only [19 km] up the Rosebud on June 22nd. On the succeeding day he made [52 km]. Then Indian signs began to show themselves and the trail became hot. On June 24th Custer marched [46 km], halted and waited for reports from his scouts. At 9.25 o'clock that night, Custer called his officers together and told them that the village of the hostiles had been located by the scouts in the valley of the Little Bighorn. It would, therefore, he said, be necessary to cross the divide between the Rosebud and the Little Bighorn. In order to [do] this without being discovered by the Indians a night march would be necessary. Three hours later the scouts informed Custer that the divide could not be crossed before daylight, so the command halted and made coffee. The march was resumed at 5 a.m., the divide was crossed at 8 o'clock and the command was in the valley of one of the branches of the Little Bighorn. Some Indians had been seen, and as all chance of surprising the village was, therefore, at an end, Custer resolved to march at once to the attack.

Commands were assigned on the march. Reno had Troops M, A and G placed under his orders; Colonel Benteen received command of Troops H, D and K; Captain

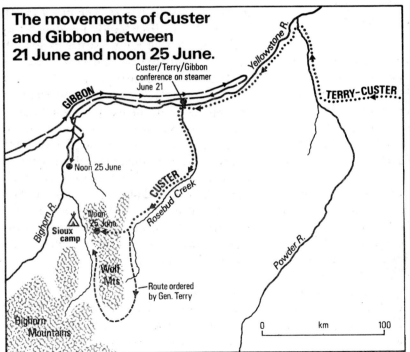

ABOVE: Indian scouts watching Custer's advance

McDougall with Troops B escorted the pack train, and Custer took with himself the fated Troops C, E, F, I and L. . . .

Reno's movements

Reno moved with [his] companies to the left of Custer's column. [Later in the afternoon] Reno [and his men] crossed the Little Bighorn, accompanied by some of the scouts, and charged down the valley [towards the village]. He finally halted in the timber and was attacked by superior numbers [of Indians]. He remained in position [for] a short time, then he thought it advisable to retreat across the river and take up a position on the bluffs. . . .

Benteen's movements

Col. F. W. Benteen, has, at the request of the author, given the following statement [about] the movements of his battalion after parting from the main command:

'I was sent off to the left several miles to hunt up some more Indians. I soon saw that the Indians had too much horse sense to travel over [that] kind of country, and concluded that 'my battalion would have plenty of work ahead with the others. Thus, I [moved] to the right to strike the tail of the main column and got into it just ahead of McDougall and his pack train.

Well, en route, I met two orderlies with messages, one for the commanding officer of the packs and one for myself. The messages read "Come on! Be quick" and "Bring packs", written and signed by Lieutenant Cooke, adjutant of the regiment. I [then] pushed to the front at a trot and got there in time to save Reno's outfit. The rest you know' . . .

Reno and Benteen are besieged

Reno, Benteen and McDougall, having [met up] fortified themselves on the bluffs and stood off the whole Indian outfit, which laid close siege to them until the 27th. Several desperate charges of the savages on the position were handsomely repulsed. . . .

'Custer's luck'?

What happened to Custer after he disappeared down the north bank of the river has been told in the words of Curley [a scout] and Horned Horse. Not an officer or enlisted man of the five troops under Custer survived to tell the tale. The male members of the Custer family, George A., Colonel Tom and Boston, were annihilated. . . .

Custer carried his battalion to the right, and moved down to the Little Bighorn valley. [Before he divided his forces] and when Custer saw all the signs of the presence of a large village, he became greatly elated. Waving his hat above his head he, according to some of the soldiers of Reno and Benteen, shouted: 'Hurrah! Custer's luck!' But luck turned its back on the hero of sixty successful charges that bloody day.

Horned Horse, an old Sioux chief, stated to Capt. Philo Clark, after the surrender of the hostiles, that he went up on a hill overlooking the field to mourn for the dead, as he was too weak to fight. He had a full view of all that took place almost from the beginning. The Little Bighorn is a stream filled with dangerous quicksand, and cuts off the ledges of the northern bluffs sharply. The Indians first saw the troops on the bluffs early in the morning, but, owing to the height of the river banks, Custer could not get down to the edge of the stream. The valley of the Little Bighorn is from [nearly 1 km] to [2 km] wide, and along it for a distance of fully [8 km] the mighty Indian village stretched.

Most of the immense pony herd was out grazing when the savages took the alarm at the appearance of the troops on the heights. The warriors ran at once for their arms, but after what seemed quite a long interval, the head of Custer's column showed itself coming down a dry water course, toward the river's edge. He made a dash to get across but was met by such a tremendous fire from the repeating rifles of the savages that his command reeled back toward the bluffs after losing several men. . . .

Custer's last stand

Horned Horse did not recognise Custer, but supposed he was the officer who led the column that attempted to cross the stream.

Custer then sought to lead his men up to the bluffs by a diagonal movement. All of them [had] dismounted, and [were] firing over the backs of their horses at the Indians. They had by that time crossed the river in thousands, mostly on foot, and had taken the General in flank and rear. Hemmed in on all sides, the troops fought steadily, but the fire of the enemy was so close and rapid that they melted like snow before it and fell dead among their horses in heaps. He could not tell how long the fight lasted, but it took considerable time to kill all the soldiers. The firing was continuous until the last man of Custer's command was dead. The watercourse, in which most of the soldiers died, ran with blood. He had seen many massacres, but nothing to equal that. . . .

Gibbon arrives

[Meanwhile] the situation of [Reno's] troops was growing desperate when the column of General Gibbon, which was accompanied by General Terry, came in sight on the morning of the 27th. The soldiers of Reno . . . at the inspiring vision, wept for joy. The Indians did not attempt any further attack after the rescuing party arrived. They, too, were tired out, and had expended a vast quantity of ammunition. They drew off toward the mountains. . . .

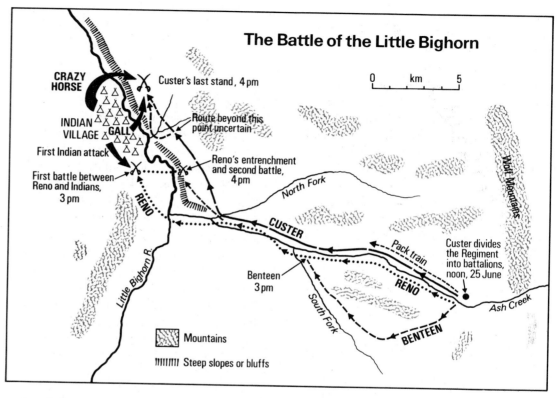

The Battle of the Little Bighorn

The 'field of blood'

General Gibbon, after a brief rest, set out to see what had become of [Custer]. General Gibbon had to march several [kilometres] before he came upon the field of blood. The sight that met his eyes was a shocking one. The bluffs were covered with the dead bodies of Custer's men, all stripped naked, and mostly mutilated in the usual revolting manner. The General's corpse was found near the summit of the bluff, surrounded by the bodies of his brothers and most of the officers of his command. The Indians, who had recognised his person, and who respected his superb courage, forebore from insulting his honoured clay by the process of mutilation. The Seventh Infantry, General Gibbon's regiment, buried the gallant dead where they

ABOVE: *Custer's last stand* by Edgar Paxson, 1899: one of the most accurate reconstructions painted after 20 years' research

fell, marking the graves of all that could be identified. Custer's remains and those of his relatives, together with those of most of the officers, have since been removed. The brave General is buried at West Point from which he graduated, and on which his glorious career and heroic death have reflected immortal luster.

J. Finerty, *War Path and Bivouac* (1890), Lakeside Classics, R. R. Donnelly & Sons, 1955, pp. 206–218

Why were Custer and his men defeated and killed?

George Armstrong Custer was probably the most dashing, glamorous and ambitious officer in the US army of the 1860s. Until June 1875 he had also been one of the luckiest. The Civil War had broken out in 1861 just as he finished his training as an officer cadet at West Point Military Academy. Despite his record number of demerits and his reputation for slovenliness, Custer's energy and reckless courage had impressed General Sheridan early in the war.

By the age of 23 Custer had been promoted to the rank of Brigadier-General, in charge of a cavalry brigade. Although when the war ended in 1865, Custer reverted to the rank of Captain, he soon began to make a reputation for himself as a daring Indian fighter in the West. In 1866 he was appointed as Lieutenant-Colonel, in effect the commander of a new

BELOW: Custer in buckskin jacket on an outing in Dakota in 1875 with Libbie and other friends

regiment, the 7th Cavalry, raised specifically for service in the West.

In 1868 Custer had distinguished himself at the Battle of the Washita. During his attack on Black Kettle's village, Custer and his men killed many warriors including the Chief, and captured fifty-three women and children. Only six men of the 7th Cavalry were lost. Time after time in the campaigns against the Kiowas and Comanches, Custer and his 7th Cavalry had emerged from battle triumphant or unscathed.

Why, then, were Custer and over half of his men killed and defeated by the Sioux at the Battle of the Little Bighorn? • Historians have argued about this question ever since 1876. Some say Custer was a hero who fought bravely against overwhelming odds. Some believe that he was unlucky and did not know he was attacking such a large Indian camp. Others, however, think that he brought about his own defeat by disobeying orders, acting rashly and disregarding the safety of his men in order to win glory for himself. Look back at the account of the battle and the events leading up to it. Next read the pieces of evidence below and try and work out some of the reasons for Custer's defeat and death.

SOURCE 132 Four views of Custer as a soldier

T. L. Rosser, a Major General in the Confederate Army in the Civil War

I have never met a more enterprising, gallant or dangerous enemy during those four years of terrible war.

General Stanley, Custer's commanding officer during the Yellowstone Expedition, 1872

A cold-blooded, untruthful, unprincipled man. He is universally despised by all the officers of his regiment.

Jacob Horner, Corporal, 7th Cavalry

He was too hard on the men and horses. He changed his mind too often. He was always right. He never conferred enough with his officers. When he got a notion, we had to go.

Theodore Ewert, Private, 7th Cavalry

The honour of his country weighed lightly in the scale against the glorious name of 'Geo. A. Custer'. The hardship and danger to his men were worthy of little consideration when dim visions of . . . a star [meaning a higher rank] floated before the excited mind of our Lieut-Colonel.

David Nevin, *The Soldiers*, Time Life Inc., 1974, p. 189

SOURCE 133 Custer in disgrace: a recent historian describes the background to certain important events which may have affected Custer's judgement before the battle

During the fall in 1875, Custer and Libbie [his wife] were savouring the delights of the big city. [At that time] a national political scandal was brewing and Custer came to play an important role.

Democrats charged that W. W. Belknap—Secretary of War—was profiteering from the revenues of traders at army posts. When the scandal over Belknap broke, Custer helped to fan the flames. . . . On flimsy evidence he accused President Grant's brother of receiving pay-offs. The testimony did not endear him to the President. . . . Grant ordered that another officer lead the Dakota column against the Indians. Custer was frantic. The chance of a life-time was ebbing away. With a new scandal in the air, the Democrats [hoped for] their first Presidential victory since . . . the Civil War. Custer may have been led to believe that with a fresh victory behind him he could be [their] candidate [for the Presidency].

With Terry's help, Custer composed a penitent telegram to Grant, asking that he be spared the [humiliation] of having his men go into combat without him . . . . Grant relented. Within a few hours of his reprieve, Custer reportedly told other officers that he would find a way to 'cut loose' and 'swing clear of Terry and run on his own'. Custer did one other thing: against orders he per-mitted Mark Kellogg a newspaper reporter for [the] New York Herald to march with the 7th Cavalry.

Nevin, *The Soldiers*, pp. 201–3

SOURCE 134 Gibbon's last words to Custer before he left the camp on Yellowstone River

'Now, Custer, don't be greedy, wait for us'. Custer's reply: 'No, I won't'.

Andrist, *The Long Death*, p. 270

SOURCE 135 Extracts from a report to General Sheridan by General Terry about the events leading up to the Battle of the Little Bighorn

While at the mouth of the Rosebud I sub-mitted my plan to Genl. Gibbon and to General Custer. It was that Custer with his whole regiment should move up the Rosebud till he should meet a trail which Reno had discovered a few days before but that he should *not* follow it directly to the Little Big-horn; that he should send scouts over it and keep his main force further to the south so as to prevent the Indians from slipping in between himself and the mountains.

We calculated it would take Gibbon's column until the 26th to reach the mouth of the Little Bighorn and that the wide sweep which I had proposed Custer should make, would require so much time that Gibbon would be able to cooperate with him in attacking any Indians. I talked with [Custer] about his strength and at one time suggested that perhaps it would be well for me to take Gibbon's cavalry and go with him. To this suggestion he replied that without reference to the command he would prefer his own regiment alone. I offered Custer the battery of Gatling guns but he declined it saying that it might embarrass him: that he was strong enough without it. The movements proposed for Genl. Gibbon's column were carried out to the letter and had the attack been deferred until it was up I cannot doubt that we should have been successful. The Indians had evidently nerved themselves for a stand.

In the action itself, so far as I can make out, Custer acted under a misapprehension. He thought, I am confident, that the Indians were running. For fear that they might get away he attacked without getting all his men up and divided his command so that they were beaten in detail.

C. Neider, *The Great West*, Bonanza Books, 1958, p. 211

SOURCE 136 Extracts from Captain Benteen's testimony about the battle, given before a Court of Inquiry in 1879

[On the morning of June 25] Gen. Custer told us that he had just come down from the mountain; that he had been told by the scouts that they could see a village; ponies, and tepees and smoke. He gave it to us as his

BELOW: Custer's Crow scouts

belief that they were mistaken; that there were no Indians there; that he had looked through his glasses and could not see any and did not think there were any there.

... We had passed through immense villages the preceding days ... we knew there were 8 000-10 000 Indians on the trail we were following ... I knew there was a large force of Indians and knew it at the time. ...

If there had been any plan of battle, enough of that plan would have been communicated to me so that I would have known what to do under certain circumstances. Not having done that, I do not believe there was any plan. In Gen. Custer's mind there was a belief that there were no Indians nor any village.

Abstract of the Official Record of Proceedings of the Reno Court of Inquiry, Stackpole Co, 1954, pp. 135, 149, 151

SOURCE 137 The story of the Little Bighorn: some comments by Colonel W. A. Graham, Judge Advocate, US Army (retired), 1926

... When the seventh [Cavalry] left the mouth of the Rosebud on the 22nd no one had any reason to believe that Sitting Bull's followers numbered in excess of 1000-1500 warriors. ...

It was common belief that the Sioux would upon the appearance of the troops, hasten to strike their camp and escape. Nobody entertained the thought that they would stand and fight a pitched battle. That was not the Indian way; nor had the troops heretofore found it possible to operate them successfully, otherwise than by surprise attacks. An hour's warning and they were gone.

... Custer therefore was an adept in bringing off surprise attacks that crushed and paralysed resistance. ...

Terry's plan of combined operations was, however, directed towards enclosing and capturing the Indians rather than to merely ... beating them in combat.

Colonel W. A. Graham, *The Story of the Little Big Horn: Custer's Last Fight*, Stackpole Co, 1926, pp. 16-17

SOURCE 138 Custer's tactics: comments by John Finerty, war correspondent of the 'Chicago Times'

It had always been General Custer's habit to divide his command when attacking Indian

BELOW: Fighting the Sioux

villages. His victory over Black Kettle was obtained in that manner. Had Custer taken his entire regiment into the fight he might still have sustained a repulse, but would have escaped annihilation. It is always a tactical error to divide a small command in face of the enemy. This was Custer's error.

Finerty, *War Path and Bivouac*, pp. 203-4

SOURCE 139 Custer's weapons: some comments by General Charles King who was Adjutant of the 5th Cavalry in 1876

Only muzzle loaders had either white or red warriors in ... December 1866. ... Then came the decade in which, with the full knowledge if not connivance of the servants of one [government] department [the Indian Bureau], the [Indians] were gradually supplied with the latest model of repeating arms and ammunition. . . .

The red warriors . . . became possessors not only of the single-shooting rifle, as issued to our . . . cavalry, but far more effective, the Winchester magazine rifle, wherewith to pump leaden missiles into . . . our, . . . troopers—a vast advantage over their luckless foe.

Summer after summer, loading up with these modern arms, enterprising fellow citizens steamed up the Mississippi meeting their Indian customers at well known rendezvous. So too at the agencies, every brave sought to be the owner of a magazine rifle . . . 'for hunting purposes'.

. . . Just as the red man was supplied with superior weapons . . . so had he a more reliable cartridge than had been issued to . . . the Seventh. . . .

For during the following year there were Indians, employed as scouts, who told our fellows of numbers of Custer's . . . followers, on . . . 25 June, seen vainly hacking with their hunting knives at cartridge shells wedged in the heated carbine chambers.

Graham, *Little Big Horn*, pp. xxiii–xxvii

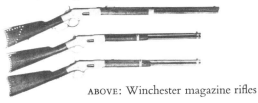

ABOVE: Winchester magazine rifles

Was the Battle of the Little Bighorn really a victory for the Sioux?

The Battle of the Little Bighorn was the US army's most decisive defeat during the Indian wars. But was it really a victory for the Sioux Indians? During the following years the Battle of the Little Bighorn proved to be a hollow triumph. The Sioux had won far too overwhelmingly, and they had won at the worst possible moment.

LEFT: Cartoon protesting against the army's shortage of money from *Harper's Weekly* 5 August 1876

When the news of Custer's defeat and death reached the American people on 6 July, they were in the midst of a time of national celebrations.

America had been an independent country for a hundred years. It was unthinkable that, at this time, the army of such a proud and successful nation should be so humiliated by the Sioux Indians. After the death of Custer, few Americans were prepared to make peace with the Indians. Instead, a large military campaign was planned to crush the Sioux once and for all. Companies of cavalry were increased from 64 to 100 men each. New recruits hurried to join the army as 'Custer's Avengers'. Army expeditions led by General Crook and Colonel Miles set out to track the Sioux in winter and in summer until they were all defeated and brought into reservations.

Black Elk later recalled the months following the battle and the effect of the army campaign on his people:

SOURCE 140 **Walking the Black Road**

We stayed in that country near the Bighorn Mountains for about a moon. My father told me all the fighting had not done any good because the Hang-Around-the-Fort people [Red Cloud and his people] were getting ready to sell the Black Hills to the Wasichu anyway, and more soldiers were coming to fight us. . . .

The flight

About this time, in the Moon of the Black Cherries [August 1876] the scattering of the people began, because by now we learned that the soldiers were coming again. Dull Knife and the Shyelas [Cheyennes] went over to Willow Creek in the Bighorn Mountains. Many of the Lakotas [Sioux] stole away in small parties and started for the agencies [reservations]. The rest of us, still a great many, started east, and the soldiers of Three Stars [General Crook] followed us. Our people set fire to the grass behind us as we went, and the smoke back there was wide as the day. This was to make the soldiers' horses starve.

Then it began to rain, and it kept on raining for days while we travelled east. Our ponies had to work hard in the deep mud, and it must have been bad for the soldiers' horses back there with nothing to eat.

Sitting Bull and Gall with some people left us and started for Grandmother's Land [Canada], and other people were going away from us all the time, but Crazy Horse would not leave the country that was ours.

After that we started west again, and we were not happy any more, because so many of our people had untied their horses' tails

RIGHT: Crook's expedition against the Sioux, 1876
BELOW: Indian prisoners

[left the warpath] and gone over to the Wasichus. We went back deep into our country and most of the land was black from the fire, and the bison had gone away. We camped on the Tongue River and a hard winter came on early. It snowed much; game was hard to find, and it was a hungry time for us. Ponies died, and we ate them. There had been thousands of us together that summer, but there were not two thousand now. . . .

The sale of the Black Hills

News came to us there in the Moon of the Falling Leaves [November 1876] that the Black Hills had been sold to the Wasichus and also all the country west of the Hills— the country we were in then. The Wasichus went to some of the chiefs alone and got them to put their marks on the treaty. Maybe some of them did this when they were crazy from drinking the minne wakan [holy water, whisky] the Wasichus gave them. But only crazy or very foolish men would sell their Mother Earth.

The attack on Dull Knife

Dull Knife was camping with his band of Shyelas on the Willow Creek in the edge of the Bighorn Mountains, and one morning very early near the end of the Moon of Falling Leaves the soldiers came there to kill them. The people were all sleeping. The snow was deep and it was very cold. When the soldiers began shooting into the tepees, the people ran out into the snow, and most of them were naked from their sleeping robes. Men fought in the snow and cold with nothing on them but their cartridge belts, and it was a hard fight, because the warriors thought of the women and children freezing. They could not whip the soldiers, but those who were not killed and did not die from the cold, got away and came to our camp on the Tongue. . . .

Dull Knife's surrender

I can remember when Dull Knife came with what was left of his starving and freezing people. They had almost nothing and some of them had died on the way. Many little babies died. We could give them clothing, but of food we could not give them much, for we were eating ponies when they died. And afterwhile they left us and started for the Soldiers' Town [Fort Robinson] on White River to surrender to the Wasichus; and so we were all alone there in that country that had been stolen from us.

Late in the Moon of the Dark Red Calf [February] Spotted Tail, the Brulé, came to us. He was a great chief and a great warrior before he went over to the Wasichus. I saw him and I did not like him. He was fat with Wasichu food and we were lean with famine. My father told me that he came to make his nephew [Crazy Horse] surrender to the soldiers, because our own people had turned against us. In the spring when the grass was high enough for the horses, many soldiers would come and fight us, and many Shoshones

and Crows and even Lakotas and our old friends, the Shyelas, would come against us with the Wasichus. . . .

'Crazy Horse untied his pony's tail'

And then I heard that we would all go into the Soldiers' Town and when the grass should appear, and that Crazy Horse had untied his pony's tail and would not fight again.

In the Moon of the Grass Appearing [April 1877] our little band started for the Soldiers' Town ahead of the others, and it was early in the Moon when the Ponies Shed [May] that Crazy Horse came in with the rest of our people and the ponies that were only skin and bones. There were soldiers and Lakota policemen in lines all around him when he surrendered there at the Soldiers' Town. I saw him take off his war bonnet. I was not near enough to hear what he said. He did not talk loud and he said only a few words, and then he sat down.

I was fourteen years old. We had enough to eat now and we boys could play without being afraid of anything. Soldiers watched us, and sometimes my father and mother talked about our people who had gone to Grandmother's Land with Sitting Bull and Gall, and they wanted to be there.

Neihardt, *Black Elk Speaks*, pp. 98-103

The defeat of the Sioux

It took the army nearly four years to defeat the Sioux. By 1880, however, most of the

BELOW: No authenticated picture of Crazy Horse exists but this is generally believed to be his photograph

roaming bands had surrendered and moved onto the reservation. In 1881 even Sitting Bull himself returned from Canada.

The Sioux had been unable to repeat their success in defeating the army at the Little Bighorn. It was impossible for such a large group of Indians to stay together for long. They would have been unable to find enough food for their families and grass for their ponies. The Indians were not used to fighting in large, organised and disciplined groups for prolonged campaigns. They preferred guerrilla warfare —lightning attacks by small bands as in

BELOW: Members of Sitting Bull's band in 1882 after their return from Canada: their tepees show how destitute they were for they are made of government canvas not buffalo hides
RIGHT: The slaughter of the buffalo

Red Cloud's war. After 1875 these small groups were no match for large army expeditions. The army was now equipped with the latest rapid firing guns and prepared to seek out the Indians even in the depth of winter.

The final blow was the destruction of the buffalo herds by white hunters. Once the Indians could no longer hunt their own food they had little choice but to move onto a reservation and take the whiteman's rations.

As time went on the Sioux reservation became smaller and smaller, and in 1876, long before all the Indians had surrendered, a commission arrived at the Great Sioux Reservation. Red Cloud and other reservation chiefs were forced to agree to the sale of a large area of their reservation including the Black Hills. The unceded Indian country granted to them in 1868 was also taken from the tribes. In 1888 the reservation was divided into six smaller reserves and the surplus land sold to the white settlers. The Sioux put up little resistance to the sale of their lands. Drought, poor harvest and epidemics of measles and whooping cough left them feeling weak in body and spirit.

The Ghost Dance and the Battle of Wounded Knee

For a short time at the end of the 1880s the Sioux began to hope for a return to their old way of life. They heard that a new Messiah was coming to save them. For believers there would be a new world. All of their dead relatives would be restored to life. The buffalo and the game would all return. All the Indians had to do was to worship the Messiah by dancing a special Ghost Dance:

SOURCE 141 **Prayer of the Ghost Dancers**

Father help us
You are close by in the dark
Hear us and help us
Take away the whiteman
Send back the buffalo
We are poor and weak
We do nothing alone
Help us to be what we once were—
Happy hunters of the buffalo.

Within a short time warriors of most of the Sioux bands had taken up the Ghost Dance. But even this ended in tragedy for the Sioux. In early December 1890 the agents became frightened and called in the army. In the panic which followed Sitting Bull was arrested and killed while trying to escape. Two weeks later 200 Sioux were shot and killed on Wounded Knee Creek by a detachment of the 7th Cavalry. This encounter became known as the Battle of Wounded Knee. The 7th

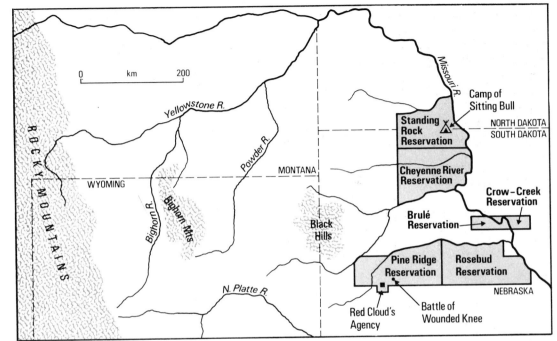

Sioux reservations in 1890-1 at the time of the Battle of Wounded Knee

BELOW: Sioux ghost dancers on the Pine Ridge reservation, December 1890
BOTTOM: The frozen body of Chief Big Foot after the Battle of Wounded Knee

Cavalry finally had their revenge for the defeat of Custer at the Battle of the Little Bighorn.

The Battle of the Little Bighorn: a defeat in victory

The Battle of the Little Bighorn had not only been Custer's last stand, it was also the Indians' last stand. Black Elk and Sitting Bull later recalled how the life of the Sioux had changed since that time:

SOURCE 142 Indian memories

Once we were happy in our country and we were seldom hungry for then the two-leggeds and the four-leggeds lived together like relatives, and there was plenty for them and for us. But the Wasichus came, and they have made little islands for us and the other little islands for the four-leggeds, and always these islands are becoming smaller for around them surge the gnawing flood of the Wasichus.

Neihardt, *Black Elk Speaks*, p. 18

The Indians may have won the Battle of the Little Bighorn, but in the end they lost the war.

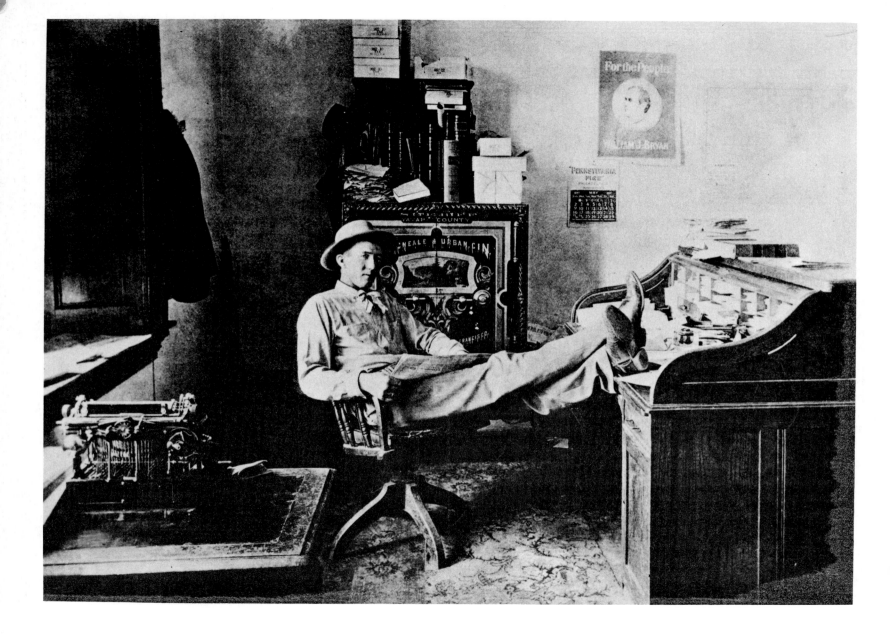

6
Government, law and order

A question of government

White settlers faced many problems when they tried to make a new way of life in the American West—lack of water, shortage of land or money, poor soil, harsh climate and in the view of many, Indians. No problem was more important, however, than that of effective government, law and order. New settlers in the West were not just concerned to provide their families with the basic necessities of everyday life —food, clothing and shelter. In the long term, they also wanted to make sure that their lives, land and homes were secure, that wills, deeds and marriages were recorded, and roads, bridges and schools built. If society in the West was not to be a 'free for all' with each man defending his own rights with a gun, then state governments and legislatures had to be established (as in the East) and officers had to be appointed to enforce the laws they made.

Federal territories

In the 1780s Congress had devised a system for organising government and land distribution in new lands in the West. When tracts of land were opened for settlement they were declared *public domain*. After survey they were divided into townships and sections (see p. 88) and sold by auction. In the early years, new areas usually did not have enough citizens and taxpayers to administer or finance a state government, legal system, roads and other services. In the meantime therefore they were organised into *federal territories*.

These territories were largely controlled and financed by the federal government. At first each territory was given a Governor,

OPPOSITE: George Ruffner, Sheriff of Yavapai county, Arizona, in the 1890s

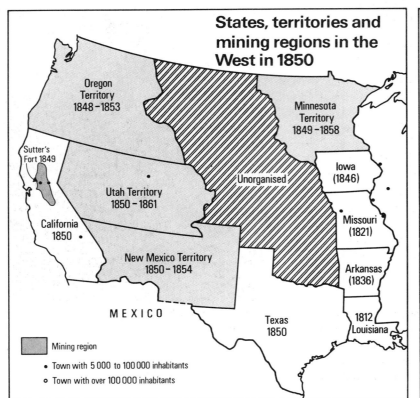

States, territories and mining regions in the West in 1850

- Oregon Territory 1848–1853
- Sutter's Fort 1849
- Utah Territory 1850–1861
- California 1850
- New Mexico Territory 1850–1854
- Minnesota Territory 1849–1858
- Iowa (1846)
- Unorganised
- Missouri (1821)
- Arkansas (1836)
- MEXICO
- Texas 1850
- 1812 Louisiana

Mining region
- • Town with 5 000 to 100 000 inhabitants
- ○ Town with over 100 000 inhabitants

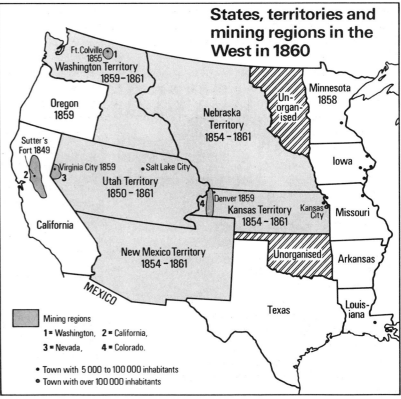

States, territories and mining regions in the West in 1860

- Ft. Colville 1855 ○1
- Washington Territory 1859–1861
- Oregon 1859
- Sutter's Fort 1849
- 2
- •Virginia City 1859
- 3
- •Salt Lake City
- Utah Territory 1850–1861
- California
- Nebraska Territory 1854–1861
- Un-organised
- Minnesota 1858
- Iowa
- Denver 1859
- 4
- Kansas Territory 1854–1861
- Kansas City
- Missouri
- New Mexico Territory 1854–1861
- MEXICO
- Unorganised
- Arkansas
- Texas
- Louis-iana

Mining regions
- 1 = Washington, 2 = California,
- 3 = Nevada, 4 = Colorado.
- • Town with 5 000 to 100 000 inhabitants
- ● Town with over 100 000 inhabitants

Secretary, three judges, an attorney and a US Marshal, all appointed by Congress. When the population of each territory had reached 5000 free adult males, the inhabitants were allowed limited self-government through their own elected legislature. Congress still, however, kept final control through its appointed Governor and officials. Provision was also made for local government in the territories. As settlers moved into different parts of each territory, county and in some places town governments were organised. Each had its own locally elected officials.

Law enforcement in the territories
Law enforcement in the territories was also organised on a dual system of local

and federal control. At the top of the lawmen's hierarchy was the US Federal Marshal who was appointed directly by the President of the United States. The US Marshal and his deputies operated throughout the territory. They were charged with enforcing federal laws and pursuing such criminals as mail robbers and US army deserters. These federal peace keepers were backed up by a few district judges, again appointed by the US government. At first these itinerant judges tried not only specific federal crimes but all major crimes such as murder (these were later left to state courts).

On the local level, the counties and townships also had their own lawmen. In the counties law enforcement rested in the hands of a locally-elected sheriff, aided by an under-sheriff and a group of deputies. The sheriff pursued criminals in his county area and in addition he had a whole range of more down-to-earth duties including maintenance of the county jail and dog pounds, inspection of cattle brands and selling the property of tax defaulters.

When a settlement grew big enough to acquire a town charter, the citizens were allowed to have their own peace officers. The mayor and council appointed a town marshal to act as chief of police. He usually had a small force consisting of an assistant marshal and a few policemen. He could also call on ordinary citizens in an emergency to serve as temporary lawmen. Minor offences in the towns and counties were tried by locally elected Justices of the Peace or police court judges.

As the chief concerns of the average citizen were family and local matters, the real mainstays of frontier law were the town marshal and county sheriff. Of the two the sheriff, who covered a wider area, had more power and prestige. Even so, the town, county and federal officials were expected to work together in the interests of government, law and order.

From territory to state

This system of law enforcement continued when territories eventually became states. When its population reached 60 000 free inhabitants (this population qualification was not always enforced), a territory could apply for admission to the Union as a fully fledged state. The new state would then take on responsibility for its own government and finance and would choose its own Governor. The federal government still kept responsibility for certain matters of national (as opposed to state) importance.

Problems with the system

On paper, Congress seems to have devised an orderly and effective system for organising government in developing areas of the West. In theory also the federal, town and county peace officers in state and territory formed an impressive hierarchy, seemingly able and equipped to enforce law and order in the West. In practice, however, the situation was often

ABOVE: Deputy US Marshal Joe Cheesman

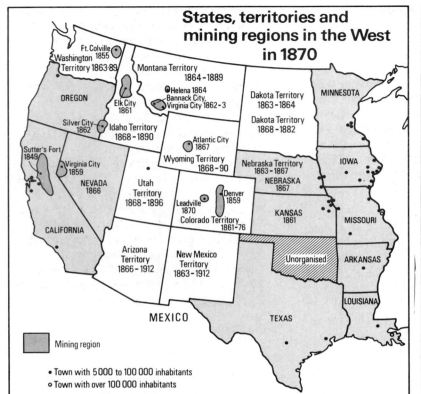

States, territories and mining regions in the West in 1870

Ft. Colville 1855
Washington Territory 1863-89
OREGON
Elk City 1861
Silver City 1862
Idaho Territory 1868-1890
Montana Territory 1864-1889
Helena 1864
Bannack City, Virginia City 1862-3
Dakota Territory 1863-1864
Dakota Territory 1868-1882
MINNESOTA
Sutter's Fort 1849
Virginia City 1859
NEVADA 1866
Utah Territory 1868-1896
Atlantic City 1867
Wyoming Territory 1868-90
Nebraska Territory 1863-1867
NEBRASKA 1867
IOWA
Leadville 1870
Denver 1859
Colorado Territory 1861-76
KANSAS 1861
MISSOURI
CALIFORNIA
Arizona Territory 1866-1912
New Mexico Territory 1863-1912
Unorganised
ARKANSAS
LOUISIANA
MEXICO
TEXAS

Mining region
• Town with 5000 to 100 000 inhabitants
○ Town with over 100 000 inhabitants

States, territories and mining regions in the West in 1890

Ft. Colville 1855
WASHINGTON 1889
OREGON
Elk City 1861
Silver City 1862
IDAHO 1890
MONTANA 1889
Helena 1864
Bannack City, Virginia City 1862-3
N. DAKOTA 1889
MINNESOTA
S. DAKOTA 1889
Deadwood
BLACK HILLS 1874
Custer City
Sutter's Fort 1849
Virginia City 1859
NEVADA
Atlantic City 1867
WYOMING 1890
NEBRASKA Enlarged 1882
IOWA
Utah Territory 1868-1896
Leadville 1870
Denver 1859
COLORADO 1876
KANSAS
MISSOURI
CALIFORNIA
Arizona Territory 1866-1912
New Mexico Territory 1863-1912
Unorganised
Oklahoma Terr. 1890-3
Unorganised
ARKANSAS
Tombstone 1878
MEXICO
TEXAS

Mining region
• Town with 5000 to 100 000 inhabitants
○ Town with over 100 000 inhabitants

very different. There was frequently a delay in establishing effective governments in new territories which covered vast areas of land. Moreover, even in new states, the system of law and order did not always function as it should. As a result problems sometimes arose.

The following sections examine two aspects of the law and order problem in the West. First we shall look at the development of government in the new mining regions of the Rocky Mountains in the 1860s. Secondly we shall study the 'range war' between cattlemen and home-steaders which broke out in the state of Wyoming in 1892.

TOP: Creede, an early mining town in Colorado

ABOVE: Miners at work

The development of government, law and order in the mining regions

Miners and their camps

In 1858-9 gold was discovered in the mountain region of the West in the future states of Colorado and Nevada, and a second gold rush began. In the following years strikes were made in many other regions (see map, p. 162). Within weeks of each find, mining camps with hundreds of people grew up. Many developed into towns as traders, cattlemen and others arrived to exploit the finds.

Early territorial government

All these camps were set up within organised territories (see map, p. 162) but there was rarely an effective government in such new areas during the early stages of a boom. Most mining camps grew up in isolated mountain regions on the far edge of vast and thinly administered federal territories (see map, p. 162). Sometimes, therefore, it was a long time before any federal officials or lawmen reached the camp. Elsewhere, as in camps around Denver (at first in Kansas territory) they were not welcomed by the miners who wanted to set up their own smaller territory (source 143). Unfortunately this process could take a long time. Though the Denver miners first petitioned Congress in 1858, the Governor of the new Colorado territory did not arrive till May 1861. The new legislature did not meet until September 1861. More time went by before laws were passed and men appointed to administer them.

SOURCE 143 **Extracts from a Colorado miner's letter**

Cherry Creek, Nov 24 1858

There are some four or five hundred men here. There is a town at the mouth of Cherry creek, with some fifty or sixty inhabitants—some three or four women amongst them; one a Mexican, one or two Mormons, and one Indian.

Men have held an election for a separate territory.

Since then, within the past few days, two men arrived here, claiming to have been sent from East Kansas, to act as sheriff and judge; with orders to lay off a county, locate a county seat, and, I suppose fill the offices to the best advantage; but by some means, the men of the town below have told them that they would not like to live under the Kansas government, and I hear threatened to tar them.

from J. S. Hardin

Leroy Hafen (ed.), *Colorado Gold Rush: Contemporary Letters and Reports 1858-9*, Arthur H. Clarke Co, 1941, pp. 170-1

The problem of land

Such delays would perhaps have created few problems in the farming areas in the eastern plains where homesteaders were scattered in isolated settlements. In the mining camps, however, things were different. There were many reasons why speedy and effective government was especially necessary here.

First, there was the problem of land and mining claims. Most early discoveries were on land that was part of the public domain. Yet between 1848 and 1866 there were no federal laws to authorise mining or to grant legal title to mineral lands. Technically speaking, therefore, miners were trespassers on the public domain without legal claim to their workings! This sometimes led to claim jumping and all the trouble which could follow (source 144).

SOURCE 144 Miners and claim jumpers in Oregon

So bold had the claim jumpers become that they openly avowed . . . to resort to violence and murder if necessary. . . . On several occasions settlers had been shot . . . and coffins were found in the post office directed to citizens, threatening them with assassination if they refused to vacate their land. Forty of the settlers now banded, armed and started in pursuit of claim jumpers.

H. H. Bancroft, 'Popular Tribunals', 1887; in V. Fisher and O. L. Holmes, *Gold Rushes and Mining Camps of the Early American West*, Caxton Printers Ltd, 1968, p. 280.

The problems of gold and desperadoes

The gold itself also created difficulties. Many of the early miners appear to have been honest and orderly men but their camps soon attracted many criminals, gamblers and prostitutes, all in search of easy gold (sources 145-6).

SOURCE 145 'Dark days in Bannack' by Granville Stuart who joined the gold rush to Montana in 1862

These were dark days in Bannack; there was no safety for life or property only so far as each individual could, with his trusty rifle, protect his own. The respectable citizens far outnumbered the desperadoes, but having come from all corners of the earth, they were unacquainted and did not know whom to trust. On the other hand the 'Roughs' were organised and under the able leadership of that accomplished villain, Henry Plummer. At times it would seem that they had the upper hand and would run affairs

BELOW: Wells Fargo reward notice

REWARD!

WELLS, FARGO & Co.'s EXPRESS BOX, on Chinese and Copperopolis Stage, was **ROBBED** this morning, by one man about two miles from Burns Ferry. (Ruplee's Bridge,) Tuolumne county side, of **$600** in coin and gold dust.

For arrest and conviction of the Robber, we will pay $300, and one-fourth of any portion of treasure recovered.

ROBBER described as follows: A Mexican, lightish complexion, rather short and thick set; weight about 150 lbs.; had a moustache and short growth of beard.

San Francisco, Dec. 1, 1875.   **JOHN J. VALENTINE,** General Superintendent.

to suit themselves. The law abiding citizens were beginning to get better acquainted and although the few attempts made to administer justice had failed they believed that the time would come . . . when the community would rid themselves of this undesirable element.

Stuart, *Forty Years On The Frontier*, Vol. I, pp. 237–8

SOURCE 146 Temptations in Virginia City (Nevada) in the 1860s

Gold was abundant, and every possible device was employed by the gamblers, the traders, the vile men and women that had come with the miners, to obtain it. Nearly every third cabin in the towns was a saloon where vile whiskey was peddled out for fifty cents a drink in gold dust. Many of these places were filled with gambling tables and gamblers, and the miner who was bold enough to enter one of them with his day's earnings in his pocket, seldom left until thoroughly fleeced.

Hurdy-gurdy dance-houses were numerous, and there were plenty of camp beauties to patronise them. There too, the successful miner, lured by siren smiles, steeped with liquor, would empty his purse into the lap of his charmer for an hour of license in her arms. Not a day or night passed which did not yield . . . fights, quarrels, wounds, or murders. The crack of the revolver was often heard above the merry notes of the violin. Street fights were frequent, and as no one knew when or where they would occur, every one was on his guard against a random shot.

N. P. Langford, *Vigilante Days and Ways*, D. D. Merrill, 1893, pp. 377–380

Problems of everyday living

Last but not least there were the problems of everyday living which resulted from the rapid and disorganised growth of the wooden shanty towns. Fire and disease (ranging from scurvy to typhoid) and bad roads were the most important (sources 147–149).

BELOW: A miners' dance
BELOW LEFT: Hurdy gurdy girls in Virginia City, Nevada

ABOVE: Helena, Montana, in the 1880s

SOURCE 147 Typhoid fever in Virginia City (Montana), 1864

Most of the miners built themselves cabins and did their own cooking. Some of these cabins were the pink of neatness while others were not so well kept . . .

There was quite an epidemic of typhoid fever during the fall and early winter and some people were very ill, but there were no deaths. The women were particularly kind, leaving their own work to . . . care for those who were ill. . . .

Stuart, *Forty Years On The Frontier*, Vol. I, pp. 266-7

SOURCE 148 The roads in Helena (Montana), described in the 'Helena Herald' 12 December 1867

One of the . . . citizens while crossing main street commenced sinking in the deep mud which filled the streets like a river . . . had the mud been a few feet deeper he would have met with the most horrible death on record.

Smith, *Rocky Mountain Mining Camps*, p. 92

SOURCE 149 Fire in Virginia City (Nevada), November 1875

Going to the door I saw the thick black smoke rolling over the hill. . . . No rain had fallen for six months, everything was like tinder. . . . The streets were filled with flying people, furniture brought out of the houses was burning on the sidewalk, . . . loose horses from the stables were dashing madly to and fro seeking to escape, with hair all burned from their backs. . . .

Lewis Atherton (ed.), 'Fire in the Comstock', in *The American West II*, Winter 1965, pp. 24-33

Miners' courts

Like most frontiersmen the miners were resourceful men and many already had experience of life in a new territory and state in California. In the absence of effective federal government therefore, they soon set up their own courts and methods of law enforcement.

The first task of the miners' courts was usually to protect the claims of the first miners in the region and arrange a fair distribution of the remaining land (source 150). The Californian miners had already developed their own *Common Law Codes* for dealing with land claims or disputes. Many Rocky Mountain miners' courts accepted or modified these same rules.

Many miners' courts also dealt with crimes, criminals and debts. When necessary a mass meeting was called and a judge and jury elected to try the case. The jury or an appointed 'sheriff' was made responsible for enforcing the verdict.

ABOVE: A miners' court

SOURCE 150 **The Bannack miners' court 1862-3, described by Granville Stuart**

The miners of Bannack met and established a miners' court. B. B. Burchett was elected judge and Henry Crawford, sheriff. A mining claim was one hundred feet [30·5 m] up or down the creek and as far out on each side as the pay dirt extended. Title to a claim was established by staking it and posting a notice and then taking it to the recorder and having it recorded. The claimant was then obliged to work his claim every day when water was available. An absence of three days constituted a forfeiture and the claim could then be jumped. In case of sickness the claim was protected until such time as the owner was able to resume work. The laws laid down by a miners' court were very simple and absolutely just. There was no appeal from the court's decision. These early day miners were men of unquestionable honesty and integrity and there was little disposition to infringe upon the rights of others, consequently the law was followed to the letter.

Stuart, *Forty Years On The Frontier*, Vol. I, pp. 232-3

Vigilantes

Miners' courts were often very effective in dealing with disputes between the miners themselves or other law-abiding citizens. Too often, however, they were powerless to prevent the serious crimes committed by road agents, robbers and other criminals who flocked into many camps. In many Rocky Mountain camps therefore, as in California, Vigilance Committees were organised. These were groups of men who met secretly and pledged themselves to work together to restore law and order (source 151). They hunted down their victims and once caught dealt with them quickly—usually by hanging (source 152).

One of the most famous Vigilante groups was the one which operated around Virginia City (Montana) in 1863. In six weeks they hanged over twenty of the worst lawbreakers and punished several more. Their work made it easier to set up a system of law enforcement when the new territory of Montana was established the following year (source 153). Other Vigilante groups, however, used their power to settle personal quarrels and came to be feared almost as much as the outlaws they hunted (source 154).

ABOVE: Vigilantes rigging gallows on a telegraph pole

SOURCE 151 Oath of the Vigilantes, Nevada City (Montana), 23 December 1863

We the undersigned uniting ourselves in a party for the laudible purpos of arresting thieves and murderers and recovering stollen propperty do pledge ourselves upon our sacred honour each to all others and solemnly swear that we will reveal no secrets, violate no laws of right and never desert each other or our standard of justice so help us God. . . .

As witness our hand and seal, this 23 of December AD 1863.

William H. Brown [and 22 other signatures]

A facsimile in Wayne Gard, *Frontier Justice*, University of Oklahoma Press, 1949, p. 180

SOURCE 152 A Vigilante hanging in Montana, described in the diary of James Miller

September 27 1865

Two men found 'hanging in the air' this morning up the gulch a little way with a card on their backs on which were the words 'Hung by the Vigilance Committee for being road agents'. The bodies were brought into town and placed in a small building where hundreds visited to get a sight of them. . . . Blue faces and open eyes looking very much like when alive.

A. F. Rolle (ed.), *The Road to Virginia City: The Diary of James Knox Polk Miller*, University of Oklahoma Press, 1960, p. 83

SOURCE 153 Professor Dimsdale's justification of the Montana Vigilantes 1865

Such was the [lawless] state of affairs when five men in Virginia [City] and four in Bannack initiated the movement [Montana Vigilantes]. In a few short weeks it was known that the voice of justice had spoken. . . . The Vigilantes . . . struck from his . . . grasp the weapon of the assassin . . . warned the thief to steal no more . . . and compelled the ruffians . . . who had so long maintained the 'reign of terror' in Montana, to fly the territory. . . .

Justice and protection from wrong to person and property are the birthright of every American citizen. . . .

These must be [provided] by constitutional law wherever . . . provision can be made for its enforcement. But when justice is powerless as well as blind . . . 'self preservation is the first law of nature'.

Prof. T. J. Dimsdale, *The Vigilantes of Montana* [first published 1866], University of Oklahoma Press, 1953, pp. 15-16

SOURCE 154 The editor of the 'Idaho World' criticises Vigilantes, 2 September 1865

A general lawlessness prevails through all these territories [Montana, Idaho, Colorado, Utah] resolving itself in the form of these [Vigilante] organisations; and everywhere they have brought trouble upon the community. . . . The remedy for the existing evils is greater than the evils. . . .

Smith, *Rocky Mountain Mining Camps*, p. 85

ABOVE: Virginia City, Nevada, in the 1870s

LEFT: A double hanging at Leadville, 1881

ABOVE: California's first jail in Monterey

BELOW: Helena jail, Montana—an example of a well-built jail

The search for legal government

Most people in the mining regions looked on Vigilantes and miners' courts as temporary stop-gap measures until proper government machinery was provided by the United States Congress. While dealing with law and order in their own fashion, the miners were usually quick to demand effective territorial government (source 155).

After the early boom, citizens in many mining camps were also keen to establish town governments (source 155). There were many reasons for this. At first it was usually lawlessness which roused citizens to demand an adequate and official police force, jail and court. Since most camps had grown up before the land was surveyed property owners were also anxious to obtain legal title to their town lots. As the months passed, however, citizens also began to demand solutions to other problems such as the provision of good roads, water supply, sanitation and a fire service. Once their town was officially incorporated they were able to appoint officials to organise all these services and raise taxes to pay for them (source 156).

SOURCE 155 New town government in Virginia City and new territorial government for Montana, described by Granville Stuart, May 1864

The new year was marvellous changes in Montana . . . we had emerged into a fully fledged territory with a population of 14 817 . . . The first territorial legislature was in session at Bannack, enacting laws for better government. Virginia City was an incorporated town: law now reigned supreme, offenders were promptly arrested and tried by authority of judge and jury. Good public schools were provided wherever six or more children could be assembled. Professor Dimsdale conducted a singing school where lovers of good music met once a week for instructions and practice.

Stuart, *Forty Years On the Frontier*, Vol. III, pp. 20–1

SOURCE 156 Mark Twain's description of Virginia City (Nevada) in 1862

Virginia [City] had grown to be the 'liveliest' town for its age and population . . . There were military companies, fire companies, banks . . . political pow-wows . . . inquests . . . a Board of Aldermen, a Mayor, a City Surveyor, a City Engineer, a Chief of the Fire Department, with First, Second and Third Assistants, a Chief of Police, City Marshal, and a large police force . . . half a dozen jails . . . in full operation, and some talk of building a church.

Large fire proof brick buildings were going up in principal streets and wooden suburbs were spreading out in all directions. Town lots soared up to prices that were amazing.

Mark Twain, *Roughing It*, Vol. II, pp. 12-13

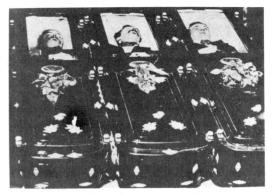

ABOVE: Tom and Frank McLaury and Billy Clanton, suspected robbers, in their coffins after their shoot-out at the OK Corral with Virgil Earp, town Marshal of Tombstone, his deputies Wyatt and Morgan Earp and Doc Holliday. After the shoot-out the Earps became increasingly unpopular in Tombstone and were accused of cold-blooded murder by some. Wyatt Earp, also a deputy US Marshal, was said to be 'little more than a tin horn outlaw operating under the protection of a tin badge . . .'

Growing pains

The establishment of government, law and order in territories and towns was not always a simple or straightforward process —even when all the officials were appointed. As a result in the early years the system did not always work very well.

County sheriffs often had to cover too large an area. Town marshals were sometimes overworked and underpaid (source 157). Some lawmen were as suspect as the criminals they were supposed to catch. In Montana, Henry Plummer the notorious road agent also doubled up as the local sheriff and appointed members of his gang as deputies (source 158).

Even when criminals were caught it could be difficult to keep them safely in flimsy jails until the trial. The court system itself also had its problems. Some judges and lawyers had an inadequate knowledge of the law and impartial juries were sometimes hard to find (sources 159-60). In areas where serious crime continued despite the establishment of territorial town and county government, citizens often resorted to Vigilante action once again (source 161). But the blame for lawlessness and delays in justice did not rest only with the officials. The local people themselves were also often at fault for paying little attention to community affairs or being unwilling to pay for an adequate police force (sources 157, 162).

SOURCE 157 A modern historian comments on the problem of law enforcement in mining towns

In spite of oft told tales, it was not a glamour job full of adventure and danger. The city marshal . . . supervised all police activities, had charge of the jail and served in such other capacities as street supervisor and dog catcher. Drunks, petty larceny, breaking city ordinances, stray dogs . . . took up most of his time. The salary varied, but was never very high. It was not unusual for the police to receive part of the collected fines . . . to supplement their income. Some camps even insisted that the men furnish a uniform at their own expense, while the town provided only the star, club and whistle. For this reward the tax payers expected a virtual superman, on the spot wherever trouble occurred and available at all times. If the community failed to provide enough money to support two shifts, either day or nightime remained unpatrolled.

The basic problem . . . was money. Far too often the public exhibited a tendency at the wrong time to be penny wise and pound foolish. Nor was community support always what it should have been. Certain people were willing to wink at infractions of the law if it meant profit. . . . Without public support, the law enforcement officers were powerless to stem the criminal element.

Smith, *Rocky Mountain Mining Camps*, pp. 122–3

SOURCE 158 The story of Henry Plummer, sheriff and highway robber, Montana 1864

The wonderful discoveries of gold at Alder Gulch attracted a large number of the dangerous class. They quickly organised themselves into a secret body of road agents, who became the terror of the whole country.

To illustrate this class of desperadoes we will take the case of Henry Plummer, a man of such smooth manners that he was termed 'a perfect gentleman', although known to be both thief and assassin. He drifted to Nevada, and, while sheriff, murdered a German in cold blood, whose wife he had first seduced. Sent to prison for this crime, but finally released by pardon, on the road he distinguished himself by stealing a horse and murdering another man, and finally found his way to Montana.

Plummer, who had been chosen chief of the 'Road Agents' Band', had likewise succeeded in having himself elected sheriff of Beaver county and appointed two of the 'band' his deputies. And all this in spite of his well-known character. In the meantime an honest man had been elected sheriff at Virginia [City], and was informed by Plummer that he 'would live much longer if he resigned his office in his favor'. Fear of assassination compelled him to do as bidden, and Plummer became sheriff at both places. One of the sheriff's deputies was an honest man, and becoming too well versed in the doings of Plummer and associates was sentenced to death by the road agents, and publicly shot by three of the band.

BELOW: Judge Roy Bean, 'Law West of the Pecos and Ice Beer'

There was no longer any security of life or property. Men dared not go outside of Virginia after dark, nor risk their lives by informing upon those who had robbed or wounded them on the highway. Inhuman murders occurred each day. . . .

John W. Clampitt, *Echoes from the Rocky Mountains*, Belford, Clark & Co, 1889, pp. 494 ff

SOURCE 159 The editor of the 'Idaho World' criticises a local Justice of the Peace

Wm Fagan, late a Justice of the Peace, ran off . . . and left divers debts . . . which he not only failed to liquidate but lied awfully to deceive his victimised creditors. . . .

But worse than this the rogue either hid or destroyed his office record book. . . . It is known that he was guilty of most shameful and even criminal acts in his official capacity. . . . He is a bad man and a cheap rascal.

Fisher and Holmes, *Gold Rushes and Mining Camps of the Early American West*, p. 294

SOURCE 160 Criticisms of the jury system by Professor Dimsdale of Montana, 1865

Another powerful incentive to wrong doing is the absolute nullity of the civil law. No matter what may be the proof, if the criminal is well liked in the community 'Not Guilty' is almost certain to be the verdict of the jury despite the efforts of Judge and prosecutor.

One grand jury that we [know] of, presented that it would be better to leave the punishment of offenders to the Vigilantes who always acted impartially, and who would not permit the escape of proved criminals. . . .

Dimsdale, *Vigilantes of Montana*, p. 13

SOURCE 161 The Virginia City Vigilance Committee announces its revival in the 'Montana Post', 23 September 1865

To all who it may concern: whereas . . . foul crimes . . . against persons and property of the Citizens of Montana have lately been committed and whereas the power of the civil authorities, though exerted to its full extent, is frequently insufficient to prevent [crime] and to punish the perpetrators . . . now this is to warn . . . that the Vigilance Committee . . . have determined to take these matters into their own hands and to

BELOW: Judge, attorney and aides at Tombstone's court in the 1880s

inflict summary punishment upon . . . all malefactors in every case where the civil authorities are unable to enforce proper penalty of the law. . . .

Gard, *Frontier Justice*, pp. 184-5

SOURCE 162 Governor William J. McConnell criticises the citizens of the Idaho mining towns

If the first settlers of Idaho . . . had directed their energies not only to making money but also to public affairs, including the election of good men to fill the offices, life and property might have been safe from the beginning as in older and well regulated states and territories.

William J. McConnell, *Early History of Idaho*, Caxton Printers, 1913, p. 254

TOP: Vigilante hangings at Yreka, California, 1895
ABOVE: Cattle rustlers

Law and order at last

Most camps went through this period of growing pains. In time, however, as systems of government and law enforcement became well established and the influence of the 'solid citizens' grew, most mining towns became orderly communities. Many townspeople became interested in all aspects of town government, including sanitation and water schemes. As one historian has pointed out, this was to the benefit of most citizens, 'a camp which presented a lawful governed image was more likely to attract permanent business and residents than one that did not'.

The Johnson County War, 1892

War in Wyoming

Problems of government, law and order were not unique to mining camps in new territories; they also existed in cattle country in recently established states like Wyoming. Wyoming was organised as a territory in 1868. In 1890 it became a state of the Union. By this time Wyoming had an established system of government and law enforcement. According to the 1890 census it also had a smaller number of criminals per million people than many older and bigger states. As one contemporary wrote, 'The great mass of Wyoming's population is made up of honest men and women as the . . . figures from the census . . . establish. . . .' Wyoming was proud of its record.

Yet within two years of statehood, a range war had broken out between cattlemen and homesteaders. The court system had failed to bring the real culprits to justice, and federal troops were quartered in two counties to ensure peace. Why and how did this violent conflict develop?

The problem in Wyoming was not that it lacked a system of government or that it was plagued by organised criminal bands. The trouble began when the community became divided into two opposing groups and each group gained influence over one part of the governmental system and used it to its own ends. In time it became impossible for either side to obtain 'justice' as they saw it. One side tried to solve the situation by taking the law into their own hands and the result was the Johnson County War.

The origins of the conflict

Trouble between the cattlemen and the homesteaders had been brewing for some time. The basic causes of the conflict were land and power. The cattlemen were the first white settlers in Wyoming. In the 1870s they had taken control of vast sections of the public domain to graze their cattle. They also gained great influence not only in the territorial legislature but also in the US Congress. Through their Stock Growers' Association the cattlemen virtually controlled territorial financial policy and obtained many laws in their own interest.

In the late 1880s things began to change: homesteaders began to settle in Wyoming. They acquired legal title to land around many water holes and began to fence off their sections. When the cattlemen started to bring pressure against them, the homesteaders began to look for some form of political power of their own. In many counties the homesteaders gained power through the jury system and the election of sympathetic sheriffs.

The immediate cause of the Johnson County War, however, was the issue of cattle rustling.

The cattlemen's case

For some time the cattlemen had been troubled by cattle rustlers, and the homesteaders were, in their view, the chief culprits.

TOP: Conflict between cattlemen and homesteaders also led to wire cutting wars in the 1880s. This photograph is a re-enactment of an incident on a Nebraska ranch
ABOVE: The cattlemen's club at Cheyenne: cattle barons dressed for the races

SOURCE 163 Extract from a petition from the cattlemen to the Governor of Wyoming, 1892

... For several years the stealing and misbranding of livestock has been of frequent occurrence. [The] influence [of the stock thieves] has become so great ... as to reach the jury box and almost effectively prevent the conviction of any person charged with stock stealing. ... In Johnson County for the five years past ... there have been only 10 convictions.

In March 1892, these thieves, ... met together at Buffalo and organised [their own] roundups in violation of law. The US Marshal and his deputies who went to serve the order injunction [forbidding this] were grossly mistreated. ...

The sheriff of Johnson county openly declares his friendship for those known to be thieves . . . there exists in the district an armed combination to prevent the administration of law and justice. . . .

We therefore pray your excellency will place the district under martial law. . . .

A. S. Mercer, *The Banditti of the Plains*, 1894, University of Oklahoma Press, 1954, p. 108-11

The homesteaders' case

The homesteaders denied the cattlemen's charge and in their turn accused the ranchers of various crimes:

SOURCE 164 The cattlemen's crimes, by A. S. Mercer, a Wyoming newspaper editor in 1892

Public opinion [among the homesteaders] has settled down to the belief that the [cattlemen] conceived the rustler howl for the purpose of securing public sympathy for their future efforts to 'run the settler out' by murder, assassination and incendiarism.

The first open and murderous attack made upon the settlers by the cattlemen . . . was in the summer of 1889. . . . Defying all forms of law, ten cattlemen rode up to [Jim] Averill's store and . . . took Averill and [Ella Watson] and hanged them. . . .

When the court convened and the grand jury was called no case was made against the [cattlemen] . . . and they were discharged.

Mercer, *Banditti of the Plains*, pp. 18-19

Planning an invasion

By winter 1891 matters had reached crisis point in Johnson County. More homesteaders had been attacked. Stockmen in Cheyenne were openly saying that there were 'too many people and not enough cattle' in Wyoming. The rustling continued. In spring 1892 the cattlemen met at Cheyenne and decided on a plan to deal with the rustlers once and for all (sources 165-6).

SOURCE 165 The lynching party, by Emerson Hough, a historian of the cattle industry, 1896

Early in the spring of 1892 a number of the large cattle owners met at Cheyenne and resolved upon a general raid against the rustlers. They agreed among themselves either

ABOVE: Montana cattlemen ride away after setting fire to a ranch house hideout of rustlers

TOP: Cattlemen hanged Ella Watson ('Cattle Kate') and Jim Averill after accusing them of rustling

to kill or drive 35 of them out of the country. In this movement were several men prominent in state affairs, and a member of the legislature.

There never was a more select, or a more inefficient, lynching party started out across the plains. Two Harvard graduates were among the outfit. There was a young Englishman along to see the fun—which he saw. One of the lynchers while asleep in camp one day chanced to toss out his hand over his blankets, and displayed two large diamond rings, which he wore as part of his range costume.

The men who should have been in charge were the twenty fighting Texans, who were imported and paid five dollars a day to go along and assist in the hanging, shooting, and driving out.

The party finally numbered forty-three men. Their outfit was as perfect as money could buy. They had three wagons and plenty of cooks, and evidently intended to travel in perfect comfort.

Emerson Hough, *The Story of the Cowboy*, D. Appleton & Co, 1897, pp. 312-13

SOURCE 166 The cattlemen gain official support for their plans, by A. S. Mercer, 1892

Knowing that their . . . action was in direct . . . opposition to all law and . . . the constitution of the state, it was necessary to ascertain how those in authority would look on the matter. Acting Governor Barber, as executive of the civil government and commander-in-chief of the state militia was the first man to look after. . . .

In March Governor Barber instructed the Wyoming National Guard not to obey orders from the civil authorities [i.e. sheriffs].

Having made 'medicine' with the Governor, friendly relations were to be created with the military [i.e. US army] at Fort D. A. Russell. . . .

Presumably the US senators, Warren and Carey, need no coaching. Both were leading cattlemen. The circumstances strongly point to some kind of an understanding with the US Marshal's office at Washington, if not the highest power [i.e. the President].

Mercer, *Banditti of the Plains*, pp. 31-39

ABOVE: A photograph of the Wyoming cattlemen and their hired Texan gunfighters taken while in custody after their defeat in the Johnson County War

RIGHT: Frank Canton, former sheriff of Johnson County, was persuaded by the cattlemen to become Chief detective in their vigilante war against alleged rustlers

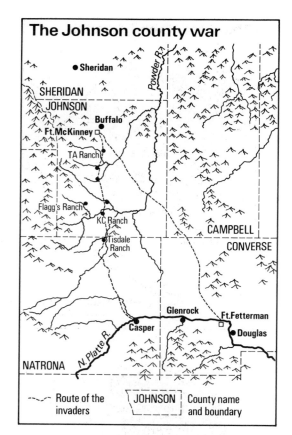

The Johnson county war

Route of the invaders

JOHNSON — County name and boundary

Invasion and war

By April 1892 the cattlemen's plans were complete and the 'invasion of Johnson County' began.

SOURCE 167 The raiders' expedition by Emerson Hough, 1896

Secretly embarking their outfit on a train at Cheyenne at night, early in April, 1892, they went by rail to Casper, Wyoming, arriving there the following night.

The siege of the K.C. ranch

The first serious business of the expedition was at the K.C. ranch, occupied by the two well-known rustlers, Nate Champion and Nick Ray. The house was surrounded by a firing party of twelve men. Presently one of the rustlers, Ray, stepped to the door, and at once fell under rifle fire. The other rustler, Champion, was finally driven out by means of fire. He was shot as he ran, and his body was left with a card pinned to it bearing the inscription, 'Cattle thieves, beware'.

While the siege of the K.C. ranch was in progress, two men came along the trail with a wagon. Owing to the poor management by the raiders, these men were allowed to escape. It happened that one of these men was Jack Flagg. Flagg was one of the prominent men accused of rustling. His escape meant the ruin of the raiders' expedition. Flagg never drew rein until he had reached the town of Buffalo. In twelve hours all Rustlerdom was alarmed and hurrying to the combat. . . .

Sheriff Red Angus to the rescue

Nor was this war upon the side of the rustlers to be without a show of legal justice. The residents of Johnson County had legally elected as their sheriff Red Angus. The sheriff had a vast posse at his back when he started forth from Buffalo to arrest the band of cattle men. From that time the invaders ceased to be the pursuers and became themselves the pursued. . . .

The battle of the T.A. Ranch

The cattlemen [at last] stopped at the T.A. ranch. Here they were surrounded by the rustlers. There were 319 men in the body which besieged the cattlemen at the T.A.

outfit. The cowmen quickly fortified the T.A. ranch, and really had things in fine shape for a long siege. The rustlers were determined to kill or capture the entire party.

While all this was going on, the commanding officer of Fort McKinney, was asked by the county authorities to assist in the capture of the cattlemen. This he declined to do, and he also declined to lend the sheriff a cannon for use against the barricaded ranch house. The rustlers then began plans for blowing up the ranch house with dynamite. . . .

The cavalry to the rescue

On the third day of the siege a troop of cavalry rode out from Fort McKinney carrying a flag of truce, to which the cowmen answered. Their surrender to the United States forces was demanded; and to this they gladly agreed on the promise that they would not be turned over to the authorities at Buffalo, which all knew meant the same thing as death. The men were finally taken by the civil authorities to Cheyenne, where they were among their friends.

Even so, far from desiring to be set free, they clung with ludicrous eagerness to their prison, and actually paid their own expenses to be allowed to remain in jail!

Hough, *Story of the Cowboy*, pp. 314-21

The end of the war

F .entually the cattlemen were brought to
court but the whole affair was a fiasco.
In the end they were allowed to go free.

SOURCE 168 No trial, no jury, by Emerson Hough, 1896

All the wealthy men of Wyoming were on the side of the cattle men, and it was foregone that they would not be convicted. When finally in court, these men were all charged with the murder of two men, Champion and Ray, and each offence made bailable in a very large sum of money. This the cattlemen were able to pay. But the Texas fighting men were not, and so, acting under advice of counsel they left the country, 'jumping' their bonds.

A list of over one thousand possible jurymen was called. By the time that half of them had been challenged it became obvious that it would be impossible to get a jury.

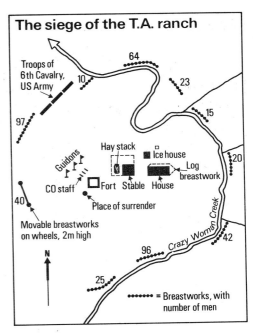

ABOVE: Sheriff Red Angus

It was actually seen that the affair was too big for the courts of the state to handle. The prosecution for the state declared that it was impossible to proceed with the cases. These men were therefore never tried, never acquitted, and yet can not be again arrested on the old charges. There are few of these cattlemen who care to speak much about this matter nowadays, and probably most of them still remain enthusiastic supporters of the law of the land today. Indeed, the law has gradually taken sway in Rustlerdom as the country has grown older.

Hough, *Story of the Cowboy*, pp. 322-3

The cost of the war

Few people were killed in the Johnson County War but it cost the cattlemen 100 000 dollars and tarnished their reputation. More important, however, it split the state of Wyoming into opposing factions. As one modern historian has commented the war 'weakened the positions of the courts, stimulated distrust of wealth and power, and created hatred and feuds that kept the people divided for generations.'

(W. E. Hollon in *Frontier Violence*, Oxford University Press, 1974, p. 161)

In the end it also marked the dividing line between the 'Old West' ruled by the cattlemen and the 'New West' of the homesteader.

TOP: Fort McKinney
ABOVE: 'What an unbranded cow has cost' from *Harper's Weekly*

Glossary

abode   home
administered   governed
administrators   government officials
adobe   unburnt, sun-dried brick
alkali   soluble salt
annuities   yearly gifts of money
aperture   opening
apostates   people who have rejected or abandoned a religious group or faith
article   custom
authenticated   proven, genuine, true
awls   small tools for pricking holes in hides (or skins)

barbarism   a savage way of life
barbarous   inhumanly cruel
basest   morally low, most cowardly
bison   buffalo
bivouac   a night camp in the open without tents
buckwheat   a kind of grain used in cooking and for animal and poultry food

calico   cotton cloth
capricious   unpredictable
chaparral   an area of stunted trees and prickly bushes
chips   animal droppings, dung
circa   about, around (when used with dates)
civil authorities   territorial, state, town or county governments (as opposed to the army—or *military* authorities)
commissary   food supply
common law codes   collections of unwritten customs and rules
commonwealth   an independent community
concur   coincide
Confederate   associated with the Southern states in the American Civil War 1861-5
conferred with   consulted

congenial   agreeable
consistency   thickness
conspicuous   easily seen, outstanding
converse   contact, conversations
cordage   ropes
corndodger   a small hard cake of corn (maize) bread
coulée   dry bed of a ravine or stream with sloping sides
creditors   people who are owed money by a debtor
Crimea   an area in southern Russia near the Black Sea

defective   faulty, inadequate
Democrats   an American political party—the opponents of the Republicans
denuded   stripped (without clothes)
depredations   attacks
designation   sign
determination   decision
diphtheria   a deadly, choking disease
divers   various
doctrine   belief, teaching

eccentric   odd, strange
edification   information, improving knowledge
emaciated   very thin and wasted
engraft   add, incorporate
en route   on the way
entrails   the bowels and intestines of animals
executive   chief official
exploits   brilliant achievements, brave deeds
extermination   complete destruction, wiping out

factions   opposing groups
fall   autumn
federal (government)   national government by Congress (as opposed to state government)

flux   liquefy, melt
forbore from insulting his honoured clay   did not insult his honoured body (i.e. mutilate)
furnish   provide

garnish   decorate
gophers   rat-like animals which live in burrows underground
gourd   a fruit like a small pumpkin

habitations   homes
Harvard   famous American university in Cambridge, Massachusetts
hides   animal skins
hierarchy   a system of organising people in graded ranks, each rank controlling the one below it
Hoyle   Edmund Hoyle (1672-1769) was famous for his book on games and their rules; 'according to Hoyle' came to mean 'done correctly'
hurdy gurdy   barrel organ

immortal luster (lustre)   everlasting glory
impetus   driving force, stimulus
incendiarism   fire raising
inconceivably   remarkably, incredibly
incorporated town   town with a legal government
infractions   breaches
ingenious   very clever at devising solutions to problems
intelligence   news
itinerant   travelling from place to place

kinship   close relationship

laudible   praiseworthy
league   a measure of distance, usually about 4.8 km
legislature   a group of people with the power to make laws (e.g. Parliament)
liquidate   pay off (a debt)
lodes   veins or seams of metal ore
lodge   an Indian's home

ludicrous   very silly
lye   a cleaning solution

maize   Indian corn or corn-on-the-cob
maladies   diseases
malefactors   evil doers, criminals
martial law   army control
merchandise   goods, wares
mesquite grass   a form of tough, thick grass which grows in very dry areas of the USA
milled   made stampeding cattle go round and round in a circle until they stopped
misapprehension   mistaken idea
molasses   dark, sweet-tasting syrup
muzzle loaders   guns which were loaded by forcing the ammunition down the barrel

nomadic   wandering from place to place with no fixed home

official capacity   official job, position

palm   prize
parflèches   raw-hide storage bags
paupers   very poor people
peck   a measure of corn, equal to about a third of a bushel
pemmican   dried buffalo meat pounded into a powder and mixed with berries
pestiferous   unhealthy, disease-ridden
pitch   a slope on a roof that enables rain to run off
plateau   flat topped mountain region, table-land
polygamy   the custom of a man having more than one wife
privation   lack of food and shelter, difficulties
profaned   wickedly ill treated; violated; treated something wholly without respect
profusion   in great numbers
prowess   bravery, gallantry

public domain   land owned by the public through the federal government
quorum   a minimum number of persons necessary for the transaction of business on behalf of some group or organisation
receptacle   container
redress   fair settlement of a grievance or injury
relapse   fall back
remuda   a group of spare saddle horses
revelation   special knowledge disclosed to a human being by God
road agent   bandit or robber (highwayman)

sadistic   very cruel
sage brush   a silvery grey shrub like a small bush 1-2 metres high which grows in very dry areas of the USA
sanction   approve
school board   group of people who manage a school
scurvy   a disease caused by lack of vitamin C which is found in fresh fruit and vegetables
sect   a religious group
sidewalk   pavement
sinews   the pieces of tough, fibrous tissue which join the muscles to the bone, tendons
siren   mythical sea nymph whose song lured sailors to destruction
sorghum   a kind of grass, like sugar-cane; syrup made from the crop
speculator   someone who buys something cheap in the hope of making a big profit when selling later
spider   an iron cooking pot with three legs
squalid   filthy
stem   hold back, stop
strategem   a trick to outwit an enemy
subsistence   food
summary   speedy

tallow   melted animal fat used to make candles
teemed   well stocked
territory   a newly settled area of the USA controlled by the federal government until it had enough settlers to organise and finance its own state government
typhoid   a fever spread by contaminated water or food

vexatious   distressing, malicious
vigil   a night spent keeping watch
violate   break, abuse

wasichus   whitemen
winked at   ignored
wrought   performed

yield   give way